THE
pregnancy
countdown
BOOK

Copyright © 2006 by Susan Magee

All rights reserved. No part of this book may be reproduced
in any form without written permission from the publisher.

Library of Congress Cataloging in Publication Number:
2005908353

ISBN: 978-1-59474-087-9

Printed in China
Typeset in Futura, Chalet, and Rockwell

Designed by Jon Barthmus @ Skidmutro Creative + Layout
Illustrations by Tina Healey

Distributed in North America by Chronicle Books
680 Second Street
San Francisco, CA 94107

10 9 8 7 6

Quirk Books
215 Church Street
Philadelphia, PA 19106
www.irreference.com
www.quirkbooks.com

THE
pregnancy
countdown
BOOK

NINE MONTHS of
PRACTICAL TIPS, USEFUL ADVICE,
and UNCENSORED TRUTHS

BY SUSAN MAGEE WITH
KARA NAKISBENDI, M.D.

QUIRK BOOKS
PHILADELPHIA

FOREWORD
By Dr. Kara Nakisbendi

One of the many things I've learned in my career as an obstetrician is that every pregnancy and birth is a unique experience. No two birth stories are ever alike.

The only similarity is that all pregnant women experience a wide fluctuation of emotions. There is great happiness and joy. But there is also doubt, worry, and anxiety. I have seen many confident women—regardless of experience or educational background—doubt their abilities to actually give birth and be a wonderful mother.

Many factors contribute to this "pregnancy neurosis"—happy one minute, scared and doubtful the next—but at its root is our fear of being completely out of control. We plan many aspects of our lives, and (if we're lucky) we'll plan the exact moment we conceive. But from that moment on, pregnant women walk a fine line between thinking we are normal and feeling like a science experiment.

Even though I'm an obstetrician/gynecologist, I had the same fears when I became a mother. I worried about the wine I drank before I knew I was pregnant. I worried that my newly implanted embryo would "fall out" if I exercised too hard. I could have used the reassuring advice that is in this book.

The key to minimizing your fears about pregnancy is to have as much accurate information as possible. There are many pregnancy books available that will give you the facts and details of pregnancy. What's unique about *The Pregnancy Countdown Book* are the emotional details. Susan Magee walks you through every stage of pregnancy, day by day. Susan makes you feel like she is reading your mind. She allows you to experience your whole range of pregnancy-induced emotions without guilt. She will even make you feel proud of them!

Just as important, she will help you keep reasonable expectations of your significant other, so that your relationship survives. You will hold onto these pages because her humor and utter clarity about the essence of pregnancy will help you feel grounded and almost normal.

It amazes me how, as women, we question all of our abilities as mothers and feel we should be doing better. No matter whether we struggled to get pregnant, experienced many losses, or suffered a medical complication during pregnancy, we all think we should have done more. With this book, Susan Magee will help you let go of that negative thinking by giving you daily words of pregnancy wisdom. Most of all, she will help you understand that you will be a great mother—because you care so much and want the very best for you and your baby!

Introduction

I'm going to tell you something about pregnancy that I wish someone had told me flat out, straight up, and early on:

Pregnancy is wonderful, joyful, and miraculous. *But it's also hard work.*

Yes, *pregnancy is hard work.*

There—it's out of the closet and onto the page. (While you have the closet door open, go ahead and put away your wine glasses, sushi take-out menu, and favorite lace undies—you won't be needing them for a while.)

I've never read a pregnancy book that is willing to go out on a limb and have the word "hard" on the first page, let alone in the entire book. Many pregnancy books and Web sites have a code word for the difficulty of pregnancy: *complex*. In my mind, carbohydrates are complex. Pregnancy is in a whole other universe of experience.

Of the many books and Web sites I've read—pregnant women can't get enough— some alluded to the difficulty by saying, "you'll have ups and downs," or "it's a tremendous change," or "you'll worry, but don't worry, you're normal." On one daring Web site, I found an article that was headlined, "No one ever said pregnancy would be easy."

Close, but that's not the same as saying it's hard.

Hard doesn't mean that you regret being pregnant. Hard doesn't mean you're not going to be a fabulous mom. Pregnancy is wonderful—very wonderful. It's also joyous, enjoyable, funny, downright doable, and yes, hard.

WHY YOU WILL COUNT IT DOWN

There's a reason why so many pregnant women become obsessed with their due dates (in fact, many will act like it was carved into a stone tablet and handed down by a bearded man in a flowing robe).

It's because your body is about to become a major science experiment—complete with all kinds of messy, gooey, itchy side effects—and your due date marks the end of it. Even better, it's the day you'll get to meet your baby.

During the next nine months, you'll have tons of doubts and questions:

"Is my baby really going to come out with ten toes?"

"Am I really going to be a good mom?"

"Will I be able to manage work and a baby?"

"Will we have enough money?"

It's hard to spend nine months with those kinds of big questions hanging over your head. So you count down the days as you head toward the answers. And you count down to all different kinds of milestones along the way.

In the first trimester—when you're likely to feel nauseated and exhausted a lot of the time—you'll be counting down to the second trimester, which is when most women start to feel better.

For women who have struggled to get pregnant, or who have had a previous loss or losses, the first trimester can be especially difficult. You may count down to every minor milestone along the way—like hearing the heartbeat and seeing your baby on the ultrasound—because your sanity depends on them.

Near the end of your pregnancy—especially if your due date comes and goes with no sign of any baby—you may start counting down the *minutes.* I've been there, and it wasn't pretty. There I was, a full two weeks overdue, wearing the only pair of shorts that still fit over my gigantic belly. None of my shoes fit by then, either, and this was especially insulting because I had bought three new pairs in my eighth month. I had to go everywhere in a pair of my husband's flip-flops. I sobbed several times a day because my cervix showed no sign of budging on its own, apparently ever.

As we've all learned from the Tom Petty song, the waiting is the hardest part. And this is especially true for pregnant women. You will wait for your first doctor's appointment, wait to hear the heartbeat, wait to have your belly show, wait to stop being sick and tired, wait for the baby to move, wait for the ultrasound, wait for people to stop touching your belly, wait for labor to start . . . It doesn't end until your doctor or midwife hands you a baby and says, "Here's your beautiful baby, and she's just fine." (Then you'll wait for the baby to take naps, but that's my next book.)

So we count down.

WE ALL JUST WANT TO BE UNDERSTOOD

This is the book I didn't know I needed when I was pregnant. Back then, I didn't have any validation for what I was feeling. A part of me was overjoyed—but another part of me, after realizing I still had weeks and months to go, just wanted to cry. I ended up getting validation much later, after meeting other moms and hearing the same things from them: "Yeah, why doesn't anyone tell you how hard it is?"

For the last year, I have talked to my friends and their friends, crashed play groups, and approached pregnant women at my son's preschool and grocery stores. I've asked all of these women what made pregnancy hard for them and what made them feel better. When you see the heading "Advice from the Trenches," I am imparting their words of wisdom directly. Most wanted their names used, but a few didn't (they're listed here as "Anonymous Mom"). But take comfort in knowing these are all real women, from many diverse backgrounds, who have been there, done that, and safely emerged from Pregnancy Land with baby in tow.

Within these pages, you will find nuggets of support, things to make you laugh, and suggestions for surviving the most amazing nine months of your life—hopefully in a cool maternity outfit or two.

THE DOCTOR I WISH I'D HAD

When my publisher asked me to collaborate with a doctor on this book, I immediately understood the wisdom of getting a medical professional involved. But I was also pretty bummed out. I had had a hard enough time finding a good doctor to deliver my son—and in many ways, giving birth to a book can be just as difficult. I thought, "How am I going to find a doctor for *this* 'baby'?" Then my sister Clare told me that I simply had to call Dr. Kara Nakisbendi. "She's amazing," Clare said. "I can just see her working on this book with you."

Kara is a mother of two young children herself, and she is indeed an amazing doctor and person—one of those rare medical professionals who calls you back right away and then makes you feel without a doubt that you are in the right hands. She's compassionate and wise, and she listens. After I recommended Kara to a friend, I asked how her appointment had gone, and my friend simply said, "Wow!" We've decided that Kara has major medicine woman in her blood.

Though this book includes some general medical information (written by Kara under the heading of "Doctor's Orders"), this information is not intended to take the place of your doctor's advice. Use it as a jumping-off point for a discussion with your own doctor or midwife. Always follow your practitioner's advice. No book, no matter how detailed, takes the place of a real medical professional. Remember your doctor or midwife is the person who knows you and your situation the best.

AND ONE MORE THING . . .

I would like to thank you for allowing me to become a part of your personal pregnancy countdown experience. If anything that is written here inspires you, makes you feel better on a bad day, gives you validation, or just makes you laugh, then I'll know this book was worth writing.

Good luck and be well on this, the greatest journey of your life: your journey toward motherhood.

THE FIRST TRIMESTER

THE WHOLE TRUTH AND NOTHING BUT
You're not even pregnant yet!

Welcome to the first countdown week of your pregnancy. Your pregnancy—and every other pregnancy—begins at day 280 and will last approximately 40 weeks. Except—guess what? At day 280, the very first day of your pregnancy, you're not even pregnant yet. In fact, you just got your period! Pretty baffling, isn't it? If you're confused, you're not alone. Read on . . .

AT THIS POINT
You've hit your first pregnancy challenge

Pregnancy is a wonderful experience, but in many ways, it's also hard. In fact, the very first thing that's hard about it is understanding exactly why a pregnancy is considered 280 days long when all of your math and calculations show otherwise. So why is your doctor or midwife going along with it? Because he or she is using the Last Menstrual Period (LMP) method of calculating the length of a pregnancy. More on that next week.

ADVICE FROM THE TRENCHES
Take the 2 weeks and run!

"Though I've had two pregnancies, I still don't understand the whole LMP business. What I do understand is that my first 2 weeks of pregnancy, when I wasn't even pregnant, are the only ones I can say were easy."
—Clare, mom to Annie and Grace

days 273–267

HOW TO UNDERSTAND THE LMP METHOD

Forget everything you think you know about when you conceived. When you think—or know—you became pregnant doesn't matter. Your doctor or midwife will always calculate your due date from the day your Last Menstrual Period (LMP) started. The main reason your pregnancy is calculated from this point and not from when you ovulated and actually became pregnant is that many women don't know for sure when they ovulated. In order to get every pregnant woman on the same calendar despite the variations in their cycles, your doctor or midwife will use the LMP date as the equalizer. So even though it's confusing to us non-medical professionals, join the confusion. The LMP is the way it works, and more importantly, this is how your due date is calculated.

DOCTOR'S ORDERS
Understand the method to the madness

"Calculating your pregnancy from your LMP is confusing, but does make sense when you consider that each time a woman has her period, her body is preparing itself for pregnancy. Doctors refer to gestational age, which is the age of your pregnancy from your LMP, and fetal age, which is the actual age of the growing baby. In general, the gestational age will always be two weeks ahead and the fetal will be two weeks behind. Most references to pregnancy are usually in gestational age rather than fetal age development, but you may see both as you read about your pregnancy."
—K.N.

days 266–260

AT THIS POINT
You may have mittleschmertzed

Mittle what?

Mittleschmertz is just a fun way to say you ovulated, or you're about to. Some women know when they ovulate, thanks to a pain called *mittleschmertz*, literally meaning "middle pain." Oh, and you did one other thing this week: You also had sex. (Now we all know. Aren't you glad your parents aren't reading this book?)

HURRY UP AND WAIT ALERT
Am I?

You mittleschmertzed, you had sex, and now you wait. And wait. And wait some more. Waiting to miss your period is your first official excursion to Pregnancy Limbo Land. You're swinging back and forth, convinced one moment that you are pregnant and the next that you're not. You may even buy a box of super tampons in a reverse jinx attempt. Only one thing is certain right now—you're on Hurry Up and Wait High Alert.

ADVICE FROM THE TRENCHES
So sure and so wrong

"You hear some women say that they knew the moment they conceived. I always thought I would know the minute I conceived. It's so special; you just think your body would know right away. When I did my pregnancy test, I was convinced it would be negative, and I was surprised to be wrong. So, you never know."
—Alexis, mom to Eva

days 259–253

THE WHOLE TRUTH AND NOTHING BUT
All trimesters are not created equal

Here's one more confusing pregnancy calendar issue to clear up. Because there are 40 weeks in your pregnancy—and forty is not equally divisible by three—you will find some variation in the length for each trimester. Some books claim the first trimester ends after week 12; others (like the book you're holding) say it's week 13; and so on. Don't worry about it. Generally, you'll know your first trimester is over when you can stay up past 7 P.M. and not vomit in the shower.

DOCTOR'S ORDERS
Recognize the early signs

"Looking for an early sign of pregnancy? After the sperm fertilizes the egg in the fallopian tube, it travels to the uterus, where it implants in the lining. At this time you may have a little spotting. This occurs around the time you are due for your menstrual period. It will most likely be dark brown blood and just a little bit, or it could be very light and mucousy. Though it doesn't happen to every woman, both are normal, and this is actually the earliest sign that you are pregnant, so congratulations!"
—K.N.

TO-DO LIST
Buy at least three pregnancy tests

When you go to get the pregnancy tests you'll soon be using, buy at least two or three. Many women, suspecting they might be pregnant, test too early, just in case. Then they'll test again, next week, just in case. Then one more time, just in case. Bottom line: You need three.

day 252

HOW TO PRONOUNCE "AMENORRHEA"

It's been one month since your last period, and now you have amenorrhea (*ah-men-or-EE-a*). It's not something you need to take antibiotics for; it's the absence of your menstrual period. For most women who didn't have spotting, this is the first sign that a baby is in the making. The big question will be answered soon.

AT THIS POINT
You can try a pregnancy test

Depending on exactly when you conceived, some home pregnancy tests may now detect the telltale human chorionic gonadotropin (hCG) hormone in your urine and give you a positive result.

The exact timing of implantation and the rise of hCG can vary from person to person, so results at this point are less than accurate—don't be surprised if your test reads negative. You'll get a much more accurate result if you wait until next week—but of course you won't be able to wait, because the suspense is killing you!

TO-DO LIST
Put the party animal out to pasture

Do yourself a big favor that will later give you tremendous peace of mind. As soon as you suspect you might be pregnant, stop drinking alcohol. Even if you're just a moderate drinker, you'll feel terrible when your doctor or midwife confirms that you really are pregnant. The same goes for other activities that are off-limits: smoking, eating sushi, refinishing furniture, changing kitty litter, horseback riding, roller coasters, and (of course) sky-diving.

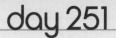
HOW TO VISUALIZE YOUR BABY

Your baby is, right now, not really a baby but a blastocyst, or a group of cells multiplying very quickly. It's hard to believe, but the person who will one day say, "I love you, Mom," is just about the size of a head of a pin.

AT THIS POINT
Your day-by-day countdown finally begins

If you have enough hCG coursing through your system, you could home test now, a day after you miss your period, and confirm that you're pregnant. If so, your countdown—the real one—starts here on day 251, just over one month from your LMP. Congratulations!

If you didn't find out you were pregnant right away and are joining the countdown late, no problem. Just count from the day your LMP started to today's date. Subtract that number of days from 280 days. This is your official countdown start day. You may want to visit that page right now and circle it. Congratulations, you're now officially in Pregnancy Land, too.

THE WHOLE TRUTH AND NOTHING BUT
You may be regretting your timing

There's no free lunch in Pregnancy Land. There's always going to be a holiday, birthday, wedding, and unseasonable weather to deal with. Look at it this way: If you're pregnant in the hot summer, it's a good excuse to hang out in a pool all weekend. If you're pregnant during the holidays, you may get waited on in stores more quickly, especially if you put your hand to your belly and say, "Ow! That one hurt!"

TO-DO LIST
Save your stick

Pregnancy is arguably the biggest event of your life, but it comes with surprisingly few mementos. You will have photographs of your ever-expanding belly, and you will have your maternity clothes. But when you're finished having children, you probably won't want to see clothes *that* big ever again—or at least for a few years—so save your home pregnancy test stick for posterity.

ADVICE FROM THE TRENCHES
Pregnancy panic

"I struggled for so long to get pregnant, and there I was, positive test in hand, in a full-blown panic about having to deliver a baby and then become a mother. I thought, 'What kind of person am I?' It wasn't until I talked to other women from my fertility support group that I realized you're still entitled to your feelings, all of them, even the doubts, no matter how long it took you to get pregnant."
—Anna, mom to Katherine

HOW TO TELL YOUR SIGNIFICANT OTHER

You will hear stories of women who buy little pink and blue bibs or rattles and wrap them up in pretty little boxes to surprise their S.O.s. Wow, so creative and patient. But if you're not the creative/patient type, don't worry. Many women will simply scream it out the window or grab the phone and start babbling. There's no right or wrong. If you want to shout, shout. You're pregnant, it's a huge deal, and you can do whatever you want.

AT THIS POINT
Am I really?

The happier you and your S.O. are about your pregnancy, the deeper and darker the doubts will be about your home pregnancy test. Maybe you screwed it up? Maybe you didn't wait long enough—or you waited too long? Maybe the box shook too much on the trip home? Though these concerns aren't completely rational, they're understandable. Everyone feels "officially pregnant" only after a doctor or midwife does a test (probably the same one you did) and announces, "You're pregnant."

TO-DO LIST
If you feel good, keep exercising

Except for sports such as scuba diving or horseback riding, and extreme sports, such as downhill racing, it's perfectly fine to keep up with most exercise programs— as long as you continue to feel okay. Just listen to your body and cut back when the good feelings stop. Talk to your doctor for more specific guidelines.

DOCTOR'S ORDERS
Believe your pregnancy is real

"This can be a very strange time. Besides missing your period and having extremely tender breasts, you may not feel all that different. It is very hard to convince yourself that the pregnancy test is correct. It is also hard to convince yourself that you won't do something to make it disappear. You may worry that if you exercise, your embryo will fly out of your uterus. I've reassured my patients that if this was really true we would not have survived as a species. No matter how educated you are, you are not protected from the awesome fears that overtake every pregnant woman."
—K.N.

THE WHOLE TRUTH AND NOTHING BUT
Your S.O.'s reaction may be disappointing

Your S.O. may not take you into his arms and lay a big kiss on your lips. Instead, he may opt for victory laps around the dining room table. This is an evolutionary impulse—the same one that makes football players jump on each other when someone scores a touchdown. This is your S.O.'s touchdown. He has implanted his seed, and he's feeling proud. Let him have his moment. He can be romantic later.

And if his joyous expression quickly turns to shock and fear, forgive him. Pregnancy is scary and shocking when you first find out about it.

ADVICE FROM THE TRENCHES
Hug with caution

"I told my husband the big news, and we were crying and hugging. I should have known that hugging for him always leads to sex. I was like, 'Are you nuts?' That was the last thing on my mind!"
—Mary, mom to Avery and Jack

AT THIS POINT
You both might be flipping out

Despite your connubial happiness, you may both be second-guessing your decision to become parents, or regretting your flimsy methods of birth control. This is the "What Have We Done?" stage of early pregnancy. Just about every couple—if they're honest with themselves—goes through this doubt and turmoil. You have just completely changed your life and your relationship—how can you not question the sanity of that?

HOW TO FIGURE OUT YOUR DUE DATE

1. Get a calendar, a pencil with a good eraser, a calculator, and some scrap paper.

2. Figure out the day when your LMP began— for example, November 20.

3. Take this day and subtract three whole months (this takes our example to August 20).

4. Add seven days. (Scientists are still trying to figure out why—just go with the flow.) In this scenario, your due date would be August 27.

5. If this makes your brain hurt, go online and search for a "due date calculator." Plenty of Web sites will do the math for you.

AT THIS POINT
Your due date rules!

Once you know your due date, it will be as if a bearded man in a flowing robe climbed down a mountain and gave you a stone tablet with that date etched on it. It's *that* big of a deal.

Pregnant women—and now you—revere their due dates for two reasons. First, this is the date when they will get to meet their beautiful babies. And second, while it's a thrill to be pregnant, it's nice to know this science experiment isn't going to last forever.

ADVICE FROM THE TRENCHES
Reality check

"Get it out of your head now that you'll deliver on your due date. You probably won't. I never did. The first time, though my doctor warned me, when the date came and went, I was crushed."

—Hope, mom to Mary, Kevin, and Vincent

day 246

THE WHOLE TRUTH AND NOTHING BUT
The "due date" scam

You know that due date you just worked so hard to calculate, the one that's now engraved in your brain? Unless there's a hurricane, a blizzard, a statewide power outage, or a nursing strike on your due date, you will probably *not* deliver your baby on that day.

Your pregnancy won't last forever, but the surprising and disappointing truth is that only one in twenty women ever deliver on their due date. Most of the other nineteen deliver after that date—up to fourteen days after, which is the longest amount of time your doctor will let you twist in the wind before inducing you.

DOCTOR'S ORDERS
Think of a "due date week"

"It can be helpful to think not of your due date, but of a due week or month. While you would think this is an exact science, doctors have no idea what the initiating factor is that causes a woman to go into labor. Since we don't know the exact moment we conceive—and given that our genetic makeup plays a role in the length of our gestations—there is a large variation in when nature says we are done. Pretty much from week 37 on is fair game. Unfortunately, most first-time mothers don't deliver until the week after their due date. It is one of the most painful first lessons of parenthood: You have no control."

—K.N.

HOW TO VISUALIZE YOUR BABY

Fruits, vegetables, and seeds are often helpful visual aids in depicting early pregnancy. Your baby is about the size of a sesame seed, or $1/16$ of an inch (1.5 mm). But don't be fooled by her tiny size; she is developing at lightning speed. Her heart has begun beating. Her brain and spinal cord are beginning to take shape. The umbilical cord—your baby's lifeline in utero—is now developing. The umbilical cord will pump oxygen, remove waste, and supply your baby with all the nutrients he needs to grow and develop for the remainder of your pregnancy.

TO-DO LIST
See the big pregnancy picture

Though right now your due date seems a very long time away, 9 months (plus 14 overdue days), you'll see how it makes not just *physical sense*—your baby has to grow body parts, after all—but *emotional sense* for you as well. There are three distinct trimesters, and they're not just for your baby's development. Some of it is about you.

You need your first trimester to get your head around your pregnancy. This is the "@&%$! I'm going to be someone's mother" phase.

You need your second trimester to feel better and bond with your baby. This is the "@&%$! There really is someone in there" phase.

You need your third trimester to get itchy, bitchy, and huge. This is the "@&%$! Just get this baby out of me, no matter how much it hurts or how long it takes" phase.

Think about it this way: Would you be ready to have a baby next month? Or even in three months? Hell, no!

DOCTOR'S ORDERS
Be prepared for bad cramps!

"Very early pregnancy can make you feel like your period is coming on—now. Period-like or even worse, lots worse, cramps are a normal and unexpected symptom of early pregnancy. Even I was surprised by how bad my cramps were. We were never taught in our residency that cramps can be normal. Imagine my surprise, and I'm the one who tells other women not to worry!"
—K.N.

THE WHOLE TRUTH AND NOTHING BUT
Oh, your aching boobs

You knew they were going to hurt or feel sore, but what is this unexpected agony? One day, probably soon, if not already, your breasts will go from really sore to extremely sore. Next, they will become those two mountains of bitter agony and regret on your chest. A comfy sports bra at bedtime and a no-touch rule are the way to go until that fire in your breasts goes out, usually during the second trimester. So hang in there, but definitely hang out in a bra for now.

HURRY UP AND WAIT ALERT
Your first doctor's appointment

You thought waiting to do your pregnancy test and waiting for the test results were hard. (Ugh. They were.) It may take you a month or even more to get your first doctor's appointment. (Ugh. That's worse.) So getting the official stamp of pregnancy from your OB/GYN is your next test of patience in Pregnancy Land.

HOW TO FIND A DOCTOR OR MIDWIFE—AND FAST

Some women interview potential OB/GYNs and midwives even before they're pregnant. If you're not that organized (or if your pregnancy was a surprise), don't worry and don't panic. Ask friends and family for recommendations. Do some research at the hospital where you plan to deliver the baby, or do some research on credible Web sites. Many hospital Web sites feature profiles of the OB/GYNs, indicating educational backgrounds, insurance info, and sometimes even childbirth philosophies.

Make at least one appointment as soon as you can. In the meantime, keep looking and get some more recommendations; at least you know you have that one appointment made.

DOCTOR'S ORDERS

Get seen early if . . .

"If you have any health conditions such as high blood pressure or diabetes, you need to let your OB know, because you will need to be seen sooner. Good blood pressure or blood sugar control in early pregnancy can ensure a healthy pregnancy. If you've had a previous loss, you will probably want to be seen earlier as well. The doctor can check your uterus and examine you and, in some cases, may give you an early ultrasound to reassure you."
—K.N.

day 242

TO-DO LIST
Ask for your prenatal prescription

When you book your first doctor's appointment, tell the receptionist or nurse that you need a prescription for prenatal vitamins. You don't want to wait on taking these—you need lots of specific vitamins, like folic acid, and minerals, like calcium, right now in specific amounts. A multivitamin from the drugstore may not have what you need. You can buy prenatal vitamins in some health stores and vitamin specialty shops, but you should check with your doctor or midwife that it has all the nutrients that you and your baby need right now.

AT THIS POINT
Communication with your doctor/midwife is key

By the time your pregnancy countdown is over, you will qualify for a Ph.D. in pregnancy. If you don't have strong opinions now about childbirth, C-sections, epidurals, episiotomies (incisions made to assist vaginal deliveries), and other aspects of labor, you might later. Therefore, the most important thing when you meet your doctor or midwife is to make sure he or she seems to be a good communicator and is open-minded. That way, as you become more educated and discover your preferences, you'll be able to discuss them with him or her.

ADVICE FROM THE TRENCHES
Finding a good practice

"When I was shopping for a good OB/GYN I made sure to find a practice that had a nurse practitioner who was available 24/7. They're so much more available than doctors, and you'll have a million questions. I called three times before my first visit."
—Cindi, mom to Justin and Cara

day 241

THE WHOLE TRUTH AND NOTHING BUT
Midwife misinformation

The biggest myth about midwives is that they don't deliver babies in hospitals. In fact, many *do* deliver babies in hospitals.

However, there are some midwives who only deliver babies in birthing centers, which are not medical facilities. Be sure to ask how the birthing center handles emergency situations and how long it takes to undergo a C-section in case you need to be transferred to a hospital.

DOCTOR'S ORDERS
Tell others when it feels right

"Patients always ask when should or can they tell their family and friends that they are pregnant. Some people ask whether it is a jinx to tell anyone while you are in the first trimester. There's no right or wrong. A good rule of thumb is: Don't tell anyone you are pregnant unless you would also tell them you had a miscarriage. You can imagine how hard it can be calling everyone if things don't go as planned. Some people like to wait until the end of the first trimester, when they have heard the heartbeat. This is when the risk of miscarriage drops dramatically."
—K.N.

day 240

HOW TO KEEP THE SECRET

If you decide to keep your pregnancy a secret for a while, here's what you need to do: *avoid* and *lie*.

Avoid your girlfriends, your sister(s), your mother, or anyone else who can see right through you.

If you can't avoid, *lie*. You can say, "No, I'm not pregnant. I'm not having wine because I've had this flu I just can't shake" or "Well that would be a miracle, considering I haven't had sex in three months." (Just don't say this one within earshot of your S.O. Others will forgive your lie later on, but he won't.)

AT THIS POINT
You've got pre-mom syndrome

If you can't keep your pregnancy a secret, blame it on your hormones.

Remember how you used to blame—with good reason—everything from your cranky mood to your chocolate binges on PMS?

Now you're probably experiencing Pregnancy Land's über form of PMS—Pre-Mom Syndrome. It starts early in your pregnancy and lasts for several weeks, usually through the first trimester. It resurfaces in the third trimester, but at least you get a break for several weeks. The mood swings are memorable—like PMS on steroids. You can go from happy to sad, joyful to miserable, annoyed to really annoyed at your S.O. and then in love with him, all in the span of five seconds. Whew! Try not to take your shifting moods too seriously. (Give your S.O. this advice, too. He needs it.)

day 239

HURRY UP AND WAIT ALERT
The heartbeat is a long way off

In a few days, your baby's heart starts contracting, but you don't get to hear it for several more weeks—at the earliest week 10, but usually by week 12. This is one of the toughest waits in all of Pregnancy Land, and it's hard on every pregnant woman. Once you hear the heartbeat, not only can you breathe a sigh of relief that your pregnancy is going well, you now have proof, other than how rotten you feel, that there really is a tiny person within.

TO-DO LIST
Join an electronic bulletin board

If you're having a lot of fear right now, or if you're just dying to spill about your pregnancy but are still keeping it a secret, an electronic bulletin board could be a good solution for you. You can be anonymous, you can share your feelings, and you can get lots of support. Knowing you're not alone in all of the surprising aches, pains, fear, and emotional turmoil can bring you a lot of comfort. (But don't take medical advice from anyone but your doctor.)

ADVICE FROM THE TRENCHES
Dealing with a loss

"I had two miscarriages before my first full-term pregnancy. Both times were an awful loss and a crushing disappointment. Your first thought is, 'I did something wrong to make this happen.' It took me a long time to understand it wasn't my fault; sometimes nature has a different plan than ours."
—Beth, mom to Scott

day 238

AT THIS POINT
You're 6 weeks pregnant!

It's been a whole month since you conceived—plus your 2 freebie weeks—and you're 6 weeks pregnant. By now your waist may already be a little thicker, and your pants a tiny bit tighter. But many first-time moms find they're still waiting for a visible change in their bellies.

HOW TO VISUALIZE YOUR BABY

Your baby is now just around $1/4$ inch (6 mm) long—think of a small lentil with a tail. But this is one busy legume. If you could see your baby, you'd see dark spots where her eyes and nostrils are beginning to form. Those little holes on the sides of her head are where her ears will be. Her arms and legs are now tiny buds, but by the end of this week those buds will be moving, thanks to the muscle fibers she's forming. By the end of the week, her heart will beat with a regular rhythm. Her backbone and rib bones are starting to form.

THE WHOLE TRUTH AND NOTHING BUT
The gagathon hormone

During weeks 6 and 7, the hCG hormone—the one that triggered the positive sign on your pregnancy test—may now begin to stand for *human chronic gagathon*. Thanks to a buildup of this hormone, many women start to feel queasy, nauseated, completely exhausted, and generally very crappy right around now. Some lucky women still have a few more weeks of feeling good. If you're one of them, enjoy!

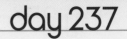
THE WHOLE TRUTH AND NOTHING BUT
Stressing out about stressing out

Stress is unavoidable, especially in early pregnancy. Major change, happy or not, is stressful. You will read that stress is bad for your baby. This just makes you more stressed, because now you're worried that you're hurting your baby. Millions of healthy and happy babies are born each year to moms who were stressed out, especially in early pregnancy. Try *not* being stressed out when you're sick and tired and your whole life has just changed! Only a Pregnancy Land-er with a bag over her head could sail through life unstressed at this point.

TO-DO LIST
Give yourself a news blackout

You can alleviate some stress just by not watching or listening to the news—so much of it is bad and upsetting, and you don't really need to know it, especially in your vulnerable state of mind. If something really big happens, you'll hear about it.

AT THIS POINT
Let the expected and unexpected symptoms begin

At 6 weeks going into 7 weeks of pregnancy, you may not yet have full-blown morning sickness, but all kinds of strange physical things may be happening to you. From here on out, any physical and psychological ailment you experience, no matter how bizarre, including but not limited to extreme moodiness, spaciness, memory loss, exhaustion, headaches, hunger, and insomnia—which of course makes you more spacey, exhausted, and emotional—*without a fever* is usually pregnancy related. In another week or two, you will have some more dramatic symptoms—like nausea and fatigue (if you don't already have them). You can't grow a person without feeling it.

AT THIS POINT
You might be reliving every cocktail you ever had

Whether it was just one glass of wine or a weekend bachelorette party extravaganza, you're going to torment yourself about how much alcohol you drank before you realized you were pregnant. If you were on any kind of medication, you are probably freaking out as well. There is never a shortage of things to worry about in your first trimester.

DOCTOR'S ORDERS
Let it go . . .

"I celebrated my birthday with several glasses of wine before I knew I was pregnant, and just like you, I regretted it. But if the pregnancy continues past the first trimester, the baby is most likely normal. This helped me get past my own worry. The most important thing is to stop any unhealthy behaviors as soon as you know and to be honest with your doctor about your fears. He or she can help alleviate your worst-case scenario thoughts."
—K.N.

ADVICE FROM THE TRENCHES
It's hard to be healthy right now

"There's so much pressure to be healthy in pregnancy, but how can you be healthy when you're an Olympic vomiter? For me, the first trimester was about feeling very unhealthy and unwell."
—Mary Beth, mom to Trevor and Justin

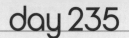

HOW TO LIVE WITHOUT ALCOHOL FOR NINE LONG MONTHS

Even if you're worried about the alcohol you drank before you realized you were pregnant, you're probably not looking forward to nine months without an occasional cocktail or glass of wine. No, you're not criminally insane; you're just a social drinker stuck in Pregnancy Land. Many moms-to-be feel this pain.

Please feel free to miss your white or red wine without shame or guilt. *Missing* is not the same as *having*. Big difference.

THE WHOLE TRUTH AND NOTHING BUT
What have I done?

It really is normal and very common to continue to feel ambivalent, scared, unsure, and even unhappy about your up-and-coming role of mom. It doesn't mean you're not happy or excited, or won't ever be, if you're not right now. You have a long road ahead of you. As far as life changes go, they don't get much bigger than this.

ADVICE FROM THE TRENCHES
Get real about your first trimester

"Go ahead and get that image of the peaceful and glowing pregnant woman with her hand on her big beautiful belly out of your head now. That is for later on. The first trimester is not about being happy. It's about getting your head around the fact that you are growing another person in your body. Even your belly can't get bigger than that."
—Wanda, mom to Tyree and Shanta

day 234

AT THIS POINT
You may be missing your other pleasures as well

No, not sex. If you're feeling sick, that's the last thing on your mind. We mean your other pleasures—all those little and not-so-little things you have to sacrifice during pregnancy: gigantic lattes, diet soda, tuna fish sandwiches, sushi, five-mile runs, and so on.

Though you gain so much in pregnancy—not just weight, but a beautiful baby at the end—you're giving up your life as you know it and have lived it. That's hard to do, even when it's for the best cause in the world.

Obviously, we know that our babies are more important than drinking a pot of coffee a day; that's why we give up our pleasures. But that doesn't mean it's not hard, and it sure doesn't mean our desire for them goes away.

ADVICE FROM THE TRENCHES
It's okay to be resentful sometimes

"There are so many adjustments you have to make in pregnancy and so much you have to give up. There were times when I resented the whole thing. Of course, that made me feel terrible. But I've learned this is pretty much how everyone feels some of the time."
—Erica, mom to Elizabeth

THE WHOLE TRUTH AND NOTHING BUT
Maternity clothes are expensive

Speaking of pregnancy resentments—start saving now for maternity clothes. Be prepared—they can be expensive.

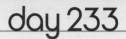

AT THIS POINT
You're suspicious of your computer

Is computer use bad for your baby? According to the Health Physics Society, even extended computer use is nothing to worry about. Visit the Web site (www.hps.org) to learn the myths and realities of other potential dangers—like airport X-ray machines (no danger unless you hop on the conveyor belt that scans luggage) and grocery store checkout scanners (no radiation involved, just a laser incapable of damaging human tissue).

THE WHOLE TRUTH AND NOTHING BUT
You're barely functional at work

Got Post-It notes everywhere? Pregnancy affects your ability to focus, concentrate, remember, and stay conscious in general. (Wait . . . what are we talking about?) Getting through work in your first trimester will be one of those things you look back on and say, "How did I do that?" But the point will be that you, like a million other working pregnant women, will somehow do it.

ADVICE FROM THE TRENCHES
Tell a trusted office buddy

"When I became pregnant, I didn't tell anyone at work except my office buddy. So whenever I became sick, she would run and call for the elevator so I could travel to a vacant floor and throw up in an empty bathroom."
—Dawn, mom to Sophia and Eva

day 232

THE WHOLE TRUTH AND NOTHING BUT
Pregnancy can feel like a job

No matter how much you love your job, you will hate working through this trimester. Pregnancy is now your real boss.

You don't want to take time off because you want to save it for later if you need it. You don't want to travel for work. (How can you make it on an airplane if you can't even get on an elevator without gagging?) You're exhausted. You don't want to work. This is pregnancy at its hardest and most unpleasant. These are the days when pregnancy feels not like joy, but hard work.

AT THIS POINT
It may help to tell your boss

You're probably wondering when to announce your big news at work. Here are some reasons why telling your boss sooner, rather than later, may be a good idea.

He or she may:

* Forgive all of the cracker crumbs on your memos.

* Not hold it against you that you're sleeping on your files rather than working on them.

* Cut you a break and let you leave early on your greenest days.

* Let you sleep on his/her couch at lunchtime.

ADVICE FROM THE TRENCHES
Some things just make sense

"There's a reason why God gives this job to women."
—Kelly, mom to Roman, Davis, Daniel, and Nadia

HOW TO VISUALIZE YOUR BABY

At 7 weeks, your baby is about the size of a blueberry—around 1/3 inch (8.4 mm)—with a short tail. Though he's so tiny, your baby's nose is already forming. Those fingers and toes you're so looking forward to counting are beginning to grow. The lenses of his eyes are developing. More and more, he's becoming recognizable as a human being and not a blastocyst.

THE WHOLE TRUTH AND NOTHING BUT
Your brain is MIA

Brain, what brain? You will forget where you put your keys, why you walked into a room, where you parked your car, and occasionally even your S.O.'s name. No, this is not a sign of early dementia. It's pregnancy-induced forgetfulness, or placenta brain, as female gynecologists jokingly call it. This is normal behavior thanks to hormones, fatigue, and the preoccupation of being pregnant. (You may even forget why you're reading this.)

AT THIS POINT
You're questioning your ability to parent

Though you can't remember where your keys are, it's likely that you can vividly recall every irresponsible, immature, and un-mom-like thing you've ever done. This is not evidence that you are going to be a bad parent; it's evidence that you're pregnant and have a lot of doubts and fears on your mind. You would be amazed at how many former party girls are now very responsible and wonderful moms. Instincts are more powerful than your past.

day 230

HOW TO EASE THE QUEASE

Let's face it, if there was a cure for "morning" sickness, we'd all know about it. You just have to try every suggested thing you hear and read about and see what happens. For some women, it's constant eating, and for others, it's figuring out what stays down. This is a difficult time of pregnancy, and you have every right to complain about it. It doesn't mean you're not happy about being pregnant. It's just no fun to be sick.

ADVICE FROM THE TRENCHES
What helped me . . .

"Don't ask me why, maybe the combination of protein and sugar, but Carnation Instant Breakfast was magic."
—Carol, mom to Ben and Gina

"Those acupressure bands worked for me. I didn't realize they were working until I took them off, thinking they weren't working."
—Natalie, mom to Brent, Hayden, and Laney

"Bananas."
—Mary, mom to Avery and Jack

"Eat anything you're craving, no matter how weird it seems, like Double Stuf Oreos for breakfast. They kept me alive."
—Bierta, mom to Craig

DOCTOR'S ORDERS
Think of sickness as a positive sign

"A helpful piece of information to get you through: Nausea and vomiting are signs of a healthy, well-established pregnancy. If you don't have these symptoms, don't despair, the opposite isn't true. You are just lucky."
—K.N.

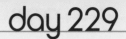

THE WHOLE TRUTH AND NOTHING BUT
Every bite counts (NOT!)

You will read this about your pregnancy diet everywhere: "When you're pregnant, every bite counts . . ."

But when you're sick, you need to eat what *you* can handle, and it's probably not going to be carrot sticks and broiled chicken. You may find yourself eating a lot more carbs right now, such as crackers, peanut butter and jelly sandwiches, and bagels.

Of course you want to eat a healthy diet—and you will, later. For now, just eat as well as you can through what for many can be a very difficult, barfy, gaggy time.

DOCTOR'S ORDERS
Get help to quit

"Many women who smoke believe that once they discover they're pregnant, it will be easy to quit. Then, to their horror and shame, they discover that it's not. Some can't seem to make the hurdle from a few a day to none a day. Nicotine is incredibly addictive, and you may need more than love and guilt to help you quit. Hypnosis can help. It's important to recognize that even if you can't seem to stop, reducing the number of cigarettes you smoke daily can have a positive impact on fetal growth. This doesn't apply if you take longer drags of the remaining cigarettes! Also, even stopping as late as 30 weeks can be beneficial to the fetus. You need to be up front with your doctor to get the help you need to stop smoking."
—K.N.

day 228

AT THIS POINT
You're wondering who coined the term "morning sickness"

There should be a "Wanted" poster in the office of every doctor and midwife, and it should read:

> **WANTED:** The not-so-brilliant guy (we know it wasn't a woman) who coined the completely inaccurate term "morning sickness."
>
> **REWARD:** You get to vomit on him at 8 P.M.

ADVICE FROM THE TRENCHES
The myth of "morning" sickness

"Morning sickness is a crock. Starting at week 6, I was all prepared with the saltines by my bedside table as instructed by my two older sisters, only to discover that it actually hit me that morning and never went away until week 16. It was actually worse in the evening before I went to bed. . . . Sickness was my biggest complaint in my first trimester with both pregnancies. I'd have to say it feels worse the first time, because you've never been through it before, and you wonder if it will ever end."
—Marianne, mom to Patrick and Andy

AT THIS POINT
Are you craving fried flounder?

No! At least, not in this trimester. A study reported in the August 1978 issue of *The American Journal of Clinical Nutrition* found that ice cream, sweets, candy (especially chocolate), fruit, and fish were the most commonly craved foods during pregnancy. Hmmmm . . . maybe the desire for fried flounder will hit you next trimester—after you stop *barfing*!

ADVICE FROM THE TRENCHES
Sexy or not?

"It wasn't until my third pregnancy that I really understood that my husband found me incredibly sexy throughout my entire pregnancy. And it wasn't until my second that he finally understood that at different points along the way, I felt nothing even resembling sexy."
—Linda, mom to William, Sean, and Hannah

AT THIS POINT
You could probably use a good laugh

But nothing is funny anymore. (Okay, one thing is funny in the first trimester; see below.) It's hard, if not impossible, to have a sense of humor when you're sick and tired and trying to deal with the idea of your pregnancy. Hang on. Your sense of humor will return in the second trimester.

THE WHOLE TRUTH AND NOTHING BUT
Sex in the first trimester?

Sex in the first trimester? Ha ha ha ha ha ha ha ha ha ha ha.

day 226

TO-DO LIST
Look up "bionic fatigue" in the dictionary

Can't remember where your dictionary is? No problem:

Bionic Fatigue *(noun)*: The excruciating and bone-crushing tiredness found in early pregnancy that is unlike any other fatigue you will experience in your life and that no one but another pregnant woman really understands. Example: "Due to her bionic fatigue, Jane leaned over to tie her shoe and woke up two hours later, barefoot and on the floor."

ADVICE FROM THE TRENCHES
Sleep anywhere soft

"I was so exhausted in my first trimester that I fell asleep on the pile of coats at my friend's Christmas party. When I came down the stairs half an hour later, my husband said, 'Where have you been and where are our coats?'"
—Karen, mom to Jenna and Kyle

THE WHOLE TRUTH AND NOTHING BUT
Exhausted one minute, wide awake the next

On the other side of the pregnancy exhaustion coin, we ironically find insomnia (hormones—the gift that keeps on giving). In fact, 78 percent of all women experience insomnia during pregnancy, and it often strikes in the first trimester. So what can you do? Call your doctor's office and ask if it's okay to occasionally use OTC remedies like Benadryl or Unisom. Many doctors will give the thumbs up if you're really not getting any sleep, but you need to call and ask first.

day 225

TO-DO LIST
Get a nap, even at work!

Thanks to your bionic fatigue, you're probably keeping your eyes open at work with paper clips. Yes, your work is important—but right now, getting a nap is more important. Here are some places to grab a quick nap.

* **An empty conference room.** Put a "Do Not Disturb" sign on the door and curl up right under the table.

* **Your car.** Just make sure you're in a safe parking lot and that a coworker knows where you are. Crack a window, lock the doors, and curl up in the backseat. (Don't leave the car running!)

* **The ladies' room.** If the ladies' room has a couch in it or even a reasonably sized chair, put a Post-It note on yourself that says, "Yes, I'm fine, just pregnant," and have sweet dreams.

* **Your desk.** If worse comes to worst, just put your head down, cover it with a file or large inter-office envelope, and grab a quick nap. It's better than nothing.

ADVICE FROM THE TRENCHES
Napping with toddlers

"I was so tired in my first trimester, I would put my son in a high chair with some toys and put a video on. Every pregnant mom I know does this. Videos and the Disney channel are the only ways to nap with a toddler in the house."
—Jen, mom to Jack and Madison

day 224

HOW TO VISUALIZE YOUR BABY

Get a tiny kidney or pinto bean and hold it in your hand. This is about the length, almost 3/4 inch (19 mm), of your baby at 8 weeks. Though she's small and you can't tell if she's really a she or a he, lots of other action is going on. Her lungs are developing, and by now, her brain has developed into five distinct areas. Though her embryonic phase will last for another two weeks, her embryonic tail is disappearing. Her torso is getting longer, and her arms and legs have lengthened. She has feet and hands, though her fingers and toes are still webbed, making them hard to count. Her head is quite large compared with the rest of her body, but her body will catch up in the next trimester.

TO-DO LIST
Put your jammies on immediately after dinner

It's a shock to many new Pregnancy Land-ers and their S.O.s when they find themselves tucked in bed and sound asleep by 8:00 P.M.—that is, if they can stay up that long. Though it feels permanent, that exhaustion you now feel really does improve, so hang in there. Tell your S.O. you'll talk to him when you wake up in the second trimester.

AT THIS POINT
Your S.O. wants to be helpful, so let him help!

If your S.O. says, "I wish I could make you feel better," tell him that a clean bathroom would make you feel better. The sad thing is, it probably *will* make you feel better.

TO-DO LIST
Go book shopping for the dad-to-be

You have this book, and probably about four hundred others to read. Your S.O. could probably benefit from some books geared specifically for expectant fathers. Warning: Some of them have a sophomoric tone—i.e., sentences like "the word *vagina* is a word you better get used to hearing a lot—ha, ha, ha." Except *vagina* is a word he *better* get used to hearing a lot as you're counting down, so if it preps him not to squirm in the doctor's office, who cares if the tone is a little immature?

ADVICE FROM THE TRENCHES
Need-to-know basis

"My husband was so loving and caring during my pregnancy, but he worried more than I did. He followed me around the house with one of my books in his hands as I drank my paltry one small cup of coffee a day saying, 'But it says right here that even small amounts of caffeine can leech calcium from the baby.' He did this until I finally screamed, 'There's only one person getting leeched, and that's me!'"
—Kate, mom to Sophie and Maggie

AT THIS POINT
Boy or girl?

You've probably heard the old wives' tale that women who have morning sickness tend to have girls. This one may actually be true. According to a study published in the medical journal *The Lancet*, women who suffer severe morning sickness early in pregnancy are more likely to have a girl. (Though many moms would tell you they were very sick and they had boys, so it's not a guarantee.)

HOW TO SWALLOW YOUR PRENATAL VITAMIN WITHOUT GAGGING

1. Tell yourself, "This is so good for my baby."

2. Put the humongous pill on the middle of your tongue (not too far back, or you might gag).

3. Take a big sip of water and immediately tuck your chin in. This is counterintuitive, but it works. The pill will automatically float to the back of your throat, and it's much easier to swallow.

ADVICE FROM THE TRENCHES
Try dissolving it

"I had to dissolve my prenatal in water first because I just couldn't swallow the pill."
—Margie, mom to Blake, Jeremy, and Robin

DOCTOR'S ORDERS
Ask for a chewable

"If you truly can't tolerate swallowing your prenatal pill, ask for a chewable one. If you can't tolerate it at all, try regular multivitamins along with extra folic acid and calcium supplements. Watch out for constipation from prenatal vitamins. The extra iron may need to be balanced out with a regular stool softener."
—K.N

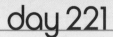

day 221

AT THIS POINT
You smell danger on the wind

While pregnant, your sense of smell will be better than a bloodhound chasing a sweaty fugitive. You will smell things you didn't know even had a smell, like the heating burners on your stovetop, exhaust from a car ten blocks away, or danger on the wind. Your super-duper sense of smell usually gets muted in your second trimester. Until then, breathe through your mouth as much as you can, hold your nose if no one's looking, and definitely ride with the car windows up and the recirculation button *on*.

TO-DO LIST
Buy an old-fashioned hanky

Just like your grandfather used to carry. If your sense of smell is making you more prone to queasiness, carry a handkerchief dabbed with a few drops of an essential oil, like lemon, which many pregnant women find agreeable. (A baby washcloth will also do the trick.) You can buy lemon oil from any natural foods store. Breathe through your scented cloth when you can't get away from an offensive smell.

THE WHOLE TRUTH AND NOTHING BUT
Another unpleasant symptom

Here's another Pregnancy Land surprise you weren't expecting—drool, especially during sleep. This is an issue for many pregnant women, especially in the first trimester, when your salivary glands are in overdrive. If you find that you're waking up in puddles, this is normal. Buy extra pillowcases while you're shopping for your hankies.

day 220

TO-DO LIST
Try some pregnancy candy or lollipops

You have to love modern civilization, especially when the result is candy made just to ease morning sickness. Here are two worth trying:

* **B-natal** is a cherry-flavored hard candy containing vitamin B6 and sugar (two ingredients found to soothe morning sickness).

* **Preggie Pops**. These lollipops come in specific flavors thought to ease morning sickness, like sour fruit, ginger, lavender, and mint.

DOCTOR'S ORDERS
Dealing with morning sickness

"At least 75 percent of women experience some form of nausea and vomiting during pregnancy to varying degrees. Many studies have shown that 10 to 25 mg of B6 vitamin three to four times a day can decrease vomiting. Some women develop regular and severe vomiting that impacts their health as well as the baby's. The most extreme form is hyperemesis gravidarum, which, fortunately, is very rare. It's very important to be aware when symptoms are getting worse and to not be afraid to seek care. This isn't a weakness! There are safe medicines that can be administered to help ward off dehydration and malnutrition."
—K.N.

ADVICE FROM THE TRENCHES
Sometimes nothing helps

"I always heard you could control the morning sickness with ginger, crackers, etc. But I learned quickly that nothing worked. If you are meant to be a 'thrower-upper' while pregnant, you will be a 'thrower-upper' regardless of how much ginger you swallow."
—Dawn, mom to Sophia and Eva

day 219

AT THIS POINT
Danger is everywhere you turn!

When you're pregnant, danger seems to be everywhere. Pregnancy in an information age can be overwhelming. As you read and surf the Web, you'll discover lots of new things to worry about—but except for really obvious dangers like smoking, alcohol, amusement park rides, saunas, and raw meat, most of the things we worry about are inconclusive or debatable. If you're nervous about manicures, microwave ovens, aerosol sprays, eating tuna fish or hot dogs, or anything else, ask your doctor for guidelines. And then try not to read too much about what's bad for you—you'll just stress and worry more.

ADVICE FROM THE TRENCHES
Don't go overboard with the boycotts

"Basically, you can worry about everything while pregnant, from blue cheese dressing to using bug spray. My rule of thumb: If it was on the list my doctor gave me of 'no-no's and if it had a smell, I avoided it. Other than that, you have to live in the real world!"
—Dana, mom to Elsie and Maya

THE WHOLE TRUTH AND NOTHING BUT
Are you dreaming of a giant baby?

Thanks to hormones, excitement, and anxiety, your dreams may now become very vivid and may sometimes feature a full-grown child instead of a newborn baby. According to Patricia Garfield, clinical psychologist and author of *Women's Bodies, Women's Dreams*, many first-time mothers dream of giving birth to fully mature babies or grown children, perhaps because they are less frightening than newborns.

day 218

THE WHOLE TRUTH AND NOTHING BUT
Is that a skunk on your head?

If you dye your hair, you've probably read the conflicting reports about the safety of hair dye during pregnancy. Even many of your favorite celebrity moms, like Sarah Jessica Parker, went back to their roots during pregnancy. But what should you do if there's a skunk on your head?

Good news, ladies. According to Dr. Connie L. Agnew in the April/May 2003 issue of *Fit Pregnancy*, today's hair dye is safe. She writes, "The Organization of Teratology Information Services, which studies substances that can cause birth defects, states, 'In animal studies, at doses one hundred times higher than what would normally be used in human application, no significant changes were seen in fetal development.'"

Whew! That's a relief. But be warned, as the article also points out: "Pregnancy hormones may change the texture of your hair, causing it to respond differently to coloring ingredients. So while it may be perfectly safe to dye your hair, you may not get the precise color you've come to expect."

ADVICE FROM THE TRENCHES
Hair salon hassles

"Even though my doctor said it was safe, I dyed my hair back to my original color as soon as I found out I was pregnant. It's hard to sit in a chair for color and highlights when you have to pee all the time. Plus, the smells from the chemicals are hard to take!"
—Emily, mom to Ryan

HOW TO VISUALIZE YOUR BABY

About 1 inch (2.5 cm), or the size of a grape or an olive. Though still small, your baby now looks more like a real human because that pesky tail is finally gone and his face is rounding out. All of his major joints—shoulders, elbows, wrists, knees, and ankles—are working and moving. His heart has divided into four chambers, and the valves have started to form. External sex organs are starting to develop, but aren't yet distinguishable as male or female.

AT THIS POINT
Your deteriorating relationship

You probably had this idea of you and your S.O. in a state of pregnancy bliss, with lots of hugs and kisses and "Love you," "No, love you more!"

And here you are, in your first trimester, exhausted, gagging, and hating him. Pregnancy *definitely* changes your relationship and certainly can strain it for a while. You're sick and tired and at the mercy of hormones, and your S.O. is sick and tired of being at the mercy of your hormones, too. You're both on the pregnancy roller coaster. Luckily, the second trimester is only five weeks away. Its arrival will renew your relationship. You really will love each other again.

THE WHOLE TRUTH AND NOTHING BUT
Your house is a mess

Your house is not getting cleaned, no cooking is going on, and there are piles of baby books all over the bed. There you are, under the covers, asleep. Looks like your house is right on schedule, too.

day 216

AT THIS POINT
Be happy you're not having a TV pregnancy

You think real pregnancies are hard? Pregnant women on TV really have it tough because they:

1. **Drop like flies.** Thankfully, fainting happens much less in real pregnancy.

2. **Give birth in cabs and on stranded elevators.** Real women usually make it to the hospital.

3. **Have an evil twin, separated at birth, who is jealous of their happiness.** Most real women have relatives who are happy for them.

4. **Have hot water boiled for them, even though no one ever seems to use it.** Real pregnant women get ice chips during labor.

HOW TO NEGOTIATE DOCTOR'S APPOINTMENTS WITH YOUR S.O.

You may have this vision of your S.O. holding the elevator door for you at every doctor's visit. He, on the other hand, may envision himself getting the doctor's and midwife's reports from you secondhand. Why? Because he's working hard at his job, which he now feels he needs more than ever in order to provide for you and the baby. He's feeling the pressure to work longer and harder.

Plus, he may feel uncomfortable being in a place where the emphasis is pretty much on uteruses and vaginas. Can you blame him?

The reality is that it might be asking too much for your S.O. to make it to every appointment. Discuss with your S.O. the key appointments—the first one, the heartbeat appointment at weeks 10 to 12, the ultrasound at weeks 16 to 20— so he can work them into his schedule early.

THE WHOLE TRUTH AND NOTHING BUT
No show, no seat

Pregnancy gives you a lot of entitlements: You get the seats on the bus, people will carry your groceries to the car—and you may even get these perks from your S.O. Pregnancy is the only time in your life when people will forgive and forget that you passed gas in a meeting or an elevator.

But, and this is really, really hard and very unjust, you don't get these benefits until you're showing. In your first trimester you'll have to tell a lot of store clerks that the reason you are drinking a six-pack of ginger ale and eating crackers in the aisle is because you're pregnant. Naturally they will look at you like, "Sure, lady, that's what all the shoplifters say."

AT THIS POINT
When will you show?

You probably won't look pregnant this entire trimester. If this is your first time in Pregnancy Land, your tummy muscles and uterus have not been stretched out before, so you'll most likely finish out the trimester with a little bit of a pot belly.

ADVICE FROM THE TRENCHES
Dealing with other people's expectations

"One of the hardest things about early pregnancy is that you feel so totally pregnant, but you don't look it yet. Therefore, your husband still expects you to cough up dinner at the end of the day, and your boss still expects you to work late. This is the time of pregnancy when you can really feel like you're in it alone."
—Dawn, mom to Sophia and Eva

day 214

THE WHOLE TRUTH AND NOTHING BUT
You still need pads

You thought you were going to get a nine-month break from sanitary napkins and panty liners, but now you feel like you've sprung a leak "down there." Though uncomfortable and annoying, increased vaginal secretions are like every other annoying surprise in Pregnancy Land—normal. The discharge is from increased hormones and blood flow to the skin and muscles around the vagina. But look on the bright side; all the lubrication will come in handy (if you know what I mean) when you get your "mojo" back in your second trimester.

AT THIS POINT
You're tired of hearing, "You're normal"

All the experts and pregnancy pundits (present company included) are telling you that every abnormal, freak-of-nature thing you're experiencing now is normal. Therefore, normal has lost all meaning. So to clarify: When people tell pregnant women they're "normal," what they really mean is, "You're not normal in the *normal*, unpregnant sense. You're normal in the *pregnancy* sense, which means nothing is normal, hence, abnormal is normal."

TO-DO LIST
Check out Lunapanties

Luna what? If you're really bumming about having to wear a panty liner or pad— and this is normal (just kidding!)—you may be a good candidate for Lunapanties. This brand of Canadian underwear is an all-in-one padded panty. You can also use them later, to deal with postpartum bleeding (www.lunapads.com).

day 213

AT THIS POINT
You may need to calm your S.O.

Your S.O. is happy and brave, too, but he has fears as well. I've divided them into two categories:

FEARS HE'LL ADMIT TO WITH SOME GENTLE PRODDING:

* **The health of the baby.** There isn't a parent who doesn't worry about this.

* **Your health.** He doesn't like it when you have to go to the hospital. It's scary.

* **Finances.** Babies are expensive. So is baby gear, baby furniture, baby diapers, baby clothes . . .

* **His ability to parent**, given that he often acts like a nine-year-old himself when around children.

FEARS HE WON'T ADMIT TO, IF HE'S SMART:

* You will never have sex with him again.

* You will get huge and stay that way—*forever*.

* You will never have sex with him again.

* You will injure him in a hormone-induced rage.

* You will never have sex with him again.

Reassurance on all counts goes a long way!

day 212

THE WHOLE TRUTH AND NOTHING BUT
Wacky pregnancy symptom #101

Many women get a terrible metallic taste in their mouths that no amount of brushing or rinsing will get rid of—a tinny tongue. This is unpleasant but not unusual. It too shall pass, most likely in the second trimester when many strange and annoying symptoms mercifully improve or disappear. Word has it that chewing ice may bring some relief, so chomp away.

AT THIS POINT
Some good news

You know those potato chips you've been craving? Turns out that potato chips actually contain folic acid. Some women do feel better eating them in the first trimester. So indulge, at least for now.

DOCTOR'S ORDERS
Don't count calories now

"You need about two hundred to three hundred more calories a day when you are pregnant, depending on where you started—but this isn't really a time to count calories. Stay away from fat-free products made with olestra. The truth is your body needs real fats (preferably good fats) to make important body parts, like your baby's brain. Try the best you can to balance out your meals. It will be much easier in the second trimester."
—K.N.

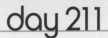
day 211

THE WHOLE TRUTH AND NOTHING BUT
Exercise? You gotta be kidding me!

There's a lot of pressure to exercise in pregnancy, because exercise is good for you. But when you're pregnant, especially in the first trimester, you have to do what feels right. Your body will guide you.

If you're one of the few women who really feels well enough to exercise for the whole first trimester, you're lucky and will be forgiven by your pregnant friends in a few years.

But if you're queasy or vomiting so much you could get a medal, or so bionically fatigued that you can't get off your sofa, you are not going to be able to exercise, and you shouldn't feel badly about it. Take the pressure off for now. You can exercise later, when you feel better.

TO-DO LIST
Freeze your gym membership

Many gyms and health clubs will let you freeze your membership for at least a month or two, especially if you tell them why (gagging can't hurt either). Freezing your membership now will help you feel less guilty about not going, because you won't be paying for it. Then when you feel better in your second trimester, you can unfreeze it. You can freeze it again later, of course.

ADVICE FROM THE TRENCHES
You may surprise yourself

"You don't know what kind of exerciser you're going to be while pregnant. I just didn't feel comfortable running or jumping. For me, walking was great exercise. And in my third trimester, going to the mall counted as a workout."
—Rena, mom to Glen

day 210

AT THIS POINT
You almost have an official fetus!

In another week, your fetal period begins. You'll be carrying an official fetus instead of an embryo. Your baby's weight can now be measured, and is just under a $1/4$ ounce (7 g). Also around now, it becomes harder to measure her total length because her legs are curled under her. An easier measurement to attain is crown to rump, or the distance from her head to her butt, which is nearly the same length as a kumquat, around $1^1/4$ inches (3.2 cm) long. Her vital organs are in place. Her eyelids are more developed, and the external features of her ears are almost fully formed.

If you visit your doctor or midwife this week, you and your S.O. may hear your baby's heartbeat for the first time—a huge relief and happy pregnancy moment because it proves your pregnancy is really real and so far, so good.

THE WHOLE TRUTH AND NOTHING BUT
You don't feel so "hottie"

On the hottie pregnant mom scale from 1 to 10, you probably feel like a –5. This week—actually this month—sorry—I mean this whole first trimester—you will probably only get to a 3, if you're lucky. You're feeling too exhausted, queasy, and hormonal to be a hottie anything. With this busy baby growing inside you, you need sleep.

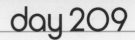
day 209

DOCTOR'S ORDERS
Don't panic about your baby's heartbeat

"Fetal heartbeats are very slippery, since your baby is still so small. At this stage, hearing it depends on luck, the angle of the instrument, and the placement of the uterus. You may hear it, and then it may fade off. Again, this is usually normal; it just means the baby has moved away, so don't panic. We don't expect to hear the heartbeat until your twelfth week."
—K.N.

HOW TO HEAR YOUR BABY'S HEARTBEAT WITHOUT FREAKING OUT

At some point in the next few weeks—if you haven't already—you can expect to hear your baby's heartbeat. While hearing the heartbeat is an amazing experience, it's also nerve-wracking. You're going to worry that you won't hear the heartbeat or that you will hear the heartbeat and something will be wrong with the way it sounds. You should know beforehand that fetal heartbeats are very fast. Your normal heartbeat is about 80 beats per minute. Your baby's normal heart rate is between 120 and 160. Also, the doctor's silence is not a bad sign—she just needs to count the beats. She also needs to differentiate your heartbeat from your baby's.

ADVICE FROM THE TRENCHES
Hearing the heartbeat

"Be prepared to not hear a calm little thumpety-thump. It sounds more like a horse galloping."
—Corinne, mom to Justin and Carley

day 208

THE WHOLE TRUTH AND NOTHING BUT
Glow? What glow?

Where the hell is that glow you've heard so much about? The misconstrued truth about the glow is this: Glowing in pregnancy is a physical thing, not an emotional or spiritual ("I am the giver of life, and I'm glowing") thing.

During pregnancy, one of the most significant changes in your body is how much your blood volume increases—on average between 45 and 50 percent. This dramatic increase in blood circulation causes your face to be brighter—at times. Those red cheeks, combined with the excess oil most women get from hormone overdrive, is the source of the glow—and pregnancy pimples—everyone talks about, expects, and will search your face for.

People see the brightness and assume it's happiness and inner peace shining out. So you expect you'll feel this radiance, too. At times you probably will. But at many, many other times during your pregnancy, just about the only thing that would make you glow would be if you put red scarves over all of the lamps in your house.

DOCTOR'S ORDERS
Hang on! Relief is coming

"Without a doubt, one of the hardest aspects of pregnancy sickness is not just the nausea and the vomiting, but the fear that it will last the whole nine months. Though some women do experience a severe form of pregnancy sickness for the duration, this is rare. It's unusual—even if you're carrying twins—to have pregnancy sickness beyond your sixteenth week of pregnancy, so hang in there."
—K.N.

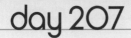

THE WHOLE TRUTH AND NOTHING BUT
Advanced maternal age label

You would think with more women becoming pregnant in their thirties and forties, the medical establishment could come up with a better term than *advanced maternal age* (AMA) to describe your pregnancy if you're thirty-five or older.

The term AMA is a throwback to when more women (our mothers) gave birth in their late teens and twenties and the oddballs were older pregnant women. The sad thing is, "Advanced Maternal Age" is the best term in the bunch. Consider some other terms for the thirty-five and pregnant set: "elderly primigravida," "post-mature," and "obstetrically senescent."

Ouch!

DOCTOR'S ORDERS
Don't let statistics get you down

"Many women believe that when they turn thirty-five their risk for having a baby with Down syndrome goes up dramatically. The truth is, age thirty-five was designated advanced maternal age for purely statistical reasons. This is the age when the risks of having a baby with a chromosomal abnormality are slightly greater than the risk of miscarrying from an amniocentesis or chorionic villi sampling (CVS). Therefore, you will be offered one of these tests, depending on how far along you are, to test for chromosomal abnormalities. What is important to hold on to is that yes, there are risks that come with having pregnancies later in our lives, but there are also technologies available to us to try to do it as safely as possible."
—K.N.

AT THIS POINT
You think *you're* AMA?

If you're over thirty-five and having a baby, here's some perspective for you. In January 2005 a sixty-seven-year-old Romanian woman gave birth to a baby girl after nine years of fertility treatments. Now *that's* AMA.

ADVICE FROM THE TRENCHES
High risk, all right

> "After getting over the shock of finding out that I was pregnant again at forty-one, I later found that I was pregnant with twins. Not only did I get strange but nosy questions from the general public, I also learned that I was 'at risk' because of advanced maternal age. 'At risk' of what? I wondered. Losing my mind? Causing my husband to have a heart attack? I was amused at most people looking at my grey 'highlights' then down to my huge belly."
>
> —Slightly older mom of Chad, Taylor, Catherine, and Isabelle

TO-DO LIST
Give yourself a new label

You don't have to consider yourself of advanced maternal age if you're over thirty-five. Choose to think of yourself as of a more confident age. You're more mature than you were ten years ago, you may have already achieved your career goals, and your partying days are way behind you. There really are some advantages to being of a more confident age and pregnant.

So don't assume you're not going to have a perfectly normal pregnancy, which of course means you'll feel anything but normal, just because of your age.

AT THIS POINT
You might be revising your future family plan

Before you became pregnant, you may have thought that three children seemed like the right amount. Now, no matter what your age, two seems more sensible. Yes, two children is definitely doable. You don't know if you could go through a first trimester twice more.

day 205

HOW TO DEAL WITH YOUR "PREGNANT" S.O.

Is your S.O. experiencing weight gain, insomnia, cravings, and morning sickness right along with you? Strange as this sounds, this happens to about 80 percent of expectant fathers. This psychosomatic condition is called Couvade syndrome, and experts believe it's caused by empathy, anxiety, or even guilt. (Depending on how you're feeling when reading this, you might be happy to learn that your S.O.'s feeling guilty.) But unless your husband tells you the baby just kicked, there's nothing to be concerned about. Even if you have your doubts, assure him that he's normal and that his symptoms will probably clear up when yours do.

TO-DO LIST
Get your S.O. to sign up for a bulletin board

Your S.O. could probably use some good old male advice to guide him through this time—so encourage him to visit a dads-to-be Internet bulletin board.

ADVICE FROM THE TRENCHES
Doctor visits with your S.O.

"After our first prenatal visit with the doctor, my husband floored me by asking me if I could switch to a female doctor. He said he felt strange being there with me knowing that another man was checking me out 'down there.' I didn't switch, and he did get used to the idea."
—Hope, mom to Mary, Kevin, and Vincent

day 204

TO-DO LIST
Sign your S.O. up for a physical

With all the emphasis on your health and the baby's health, now is a good time to get your S.O. to focus on his health and not just yours. Get him to sign up for a full physical. He's feeling vulnerable, too, and a clean bill of health can make him feel better.

HOW TO EASE THE QUEASE
With cucumbers!

If you still have the queasies—and many women do— you're probably ready to try any crazy remedy as long as it's safe. Here is one that some women swear by— cucumbers soaked in water. Let the cucumbers soak for ten minutes and then give them a try.

AT THIS POINT
Finally, a benefit of being pregnant

You may be gagging, tired, and green round the edges, but there's at least one benefit that comes from visiting Pregnancy Land: Your hair probably looks great.

It's a fact that many women experience healthier hair during pregnancy. Thanks to vitamins and hormones, you may have full and thick hair. You may also experience a complete hair reversal. Curly-haired women have gone straight and vice versa. Still, some women report that their curly hair didn't become straight but went to frizzy. At least the change can take your mind off how sick and tired you are.

HOW TO VISUALIZE YOUR BABY

At 11 weeks, your baby is quickly moving up in the pregnancy fruit bowl. By now he's anywhere from 1 1/2 to 2 inches (3.8–5 cm) long from crown to rump, about the length of a large strawberry. His skin is transparent, so his blood vessels show through. Tiny tooth buds are now appearing under his gums. His fingers and toes have separated.

AT THIS POINT
Placenta unplugged

At some point in the next week or so, the placenta, an amazing organ within your uterus that is dark maroon in color with a bumpy surface that resembles a head of cauliflower, will begin to function, providing oxygen and essential nutrients to your baby.

Even though he's inside you, your baby never directly touches your uterine wall. Two membranes—the chorion on your side and the amnion on his side—surround him with amniotic fluid. Only the umbilical cord, which enters through your baby's belly-button, penetrates both of these membranes to connect your baby to you. Exchanges of oxygen, waste products for elimination, and nutrients from your blood occur only at the place where the umbilical cord fuses with the uterine wall—the placenta.

The placenta is also called the "afterbirth" because after you deliver your baby, you deliver the placenta.

AT THIS POINT
Can a heartbeat reveal the baby's sex?

Every expert says no. And yet most experts agree that girls tend to have faster heartbeats than boys. (Girls: 140 beats per minute or higher. Boys: 140 beats per minute or lower.) But this is only a generalization; don't pick out your nursery theme based on your baby's heartbeat.

TO-DO LIST
Put the fetal heartbeat monitor back on the store shelf

Do not buy a fetal heart monitor to use at home. Repeat: Don't do it. They're expensive. They're hard to use. And you'll just horrify yourself if you don't hear anything (and you probably won't). You're better off saving the sounds for the doctor's office. Bring a tape recorder to the doctor or midwife's office and record the heartbeat for yourself. You'll never tire of listening to it.

ADVICE FROM THE TRENCHES
No part of your life is unchanged

"I'm an avid reader, at least until I got pregnant. If it wasn't a pregnancy book, I couldn't read a page and remember what I had read. I was like this for my whole pregnancy. I worried that I was going to be permanently disabled this way and never read novels again. Now, I can read again, but with two young kids, I can't read a whole lot because I don't have a lot of time."
—Mary Judith, mom to Caitlyn and Jordan

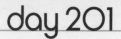
day 201

AT THIS POINT
There's a "fundus" among us . . .

. . . and it's your ever-expanding uterus. In just a few days, your uterus will rise above your pelvic bones and your doctor or midwife will be able to feel the top of it—it's called the fundus. Pregnancy is probably the only time you get to say this word, so enjoy.

HURRY UP AND WAIT ALERT
The ultrasound is ultra far away

Though hearing your baby's heartbeat means your chance of miscarriage is slim, many pregnant women still feel nervous and unsure about their pregnancies until they see the baby with their own eyes. Unfortunately, your ultrasound is still several weeks away—usually in week 16. This will be your next challenge in the great waiting room of pregnancy.

DOCTOR'S ORDERS
Dealing with your fear

"Once you have heard your baby's heartbeat, it is really hard to hold onto it until your next visit. Since you don't feel movement yet, many women get nervous since their fatigue and nausea may be improving. This is especially true if you have experienced a pregnancy loss in the past; you are going to require more visits to get through each stage. You may not be able to go four weeks between appointments without going nuts. Don't be afraid to share your anxieties and tell your doctor what you need. Having the option to come in more frequently or to come in when the anxiety is peaking will help immensely."
—K.N.

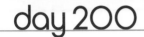

HOW TO BREAK THE BIG NEWS

When the time is right, there are two general guidelines that you may find helpful:

1. Both sets of grandparents must be notified, or led to believe they were both notified, on the same day and within minutes of each other.

2. Allow your S.O. to hike up his pants and crack the usual jokes, like: "Yes, I knew I had good swimmers." He did have at least one good swimmer, so let him get away with it.

ADVICE FROM THE TRENCHES
Get ready for the questions

"As soon as you announce the news, get ready for the questions: 'How long were you trying? Was it a surprise? Are you going to find out the sex? Are you going to have an amnio? Are you going to quit work? Are you vomiting yet?' Telling people is wonderful—but it can also be a drag. I learned that people mean well but they definitely feel entitled to know all the details of your private life."
—Christine, mom to Julie and Maddie

AT THIS POINT
Someone's feelings will be hurt

You can't win. It took everything for you to keep your secret, and now someone's upset that you didn't share your information sooner. Don't worry—that person will get over it, especially once you start calling to complain about all of your pregnancy aches and pains.

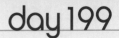
THE WHOLE TRUTH AND NOTHING BUT
Other people suck (sometimes)

People's reactions to your big news are not always what you expect. You may be hurt or disappointed because a friend doesn't seem happy for you.

Remember, the way people react to your pregnancy has more to do with them than you. Your friend may be jealous and conflicted, or she may be trying to get pregnant and is having a hard time. She may be single and feeling way behind the curve. She may be worried that her relationship with you is going to change—and she's right, it will.

AT THIS POINT
You can ignore what women over fifty-five tell you

Other women, especially the "older generation" (code words for your mother and your mother-in-law) are quite opinionated about pregnancy. Fortunately, you can ignore what any woman over fifty-five has to say. They're the ones who drank brandy to ease Braxton Hicks contractions, drove to the doctor's appointment with no seatbelt on, and had a cigarette with their pot of coffee in the morning.

ADVICE FROM THE TRENCHES
Times have changed

"I think it was easier for our mothers. They didn't have the same pressures of working and being in shape. They didn't have the pressure to be healthy. They drank their coffee and ate their tuna fish in peace. In many ways, their lives really did just go on. Ours are turned completely upside down and inside out."
—Clare, mom to Annie and Grace

day 198

AT THIS POINT
Can your baby do any tricks?

Besides making you nauseated, your baby has plenty of new and amazing tricks. He can open his mouth and close his fist. He can also suck his thumb. Sucking a thumb may not sound amazing, but consider that although he can suck a thumb, he is barely the size of yours. Pretty impressive!

TO-DO LIST
Plan for pee emergencies

Never go anywhere without: (1) Using the bathroom before you leave, even if you just went; (2) locating a new bathroom the moment you arrive; and (3) carrying plenty of tissues, just in case you need to duck behind a bush—which, believe it or not, happens to more women than you might think.

ADVICE FROM THE TRENCHES
If you gotta go . . .

"During a long car trip, I really had to go, and there wasn't a bush or tree for miles. My husband pulled over, I scooted up to end of my seat, took my soda cup, and peed in it. After that, I never went anywhere without a big plastic container with a lid."
—Susie, mom to Devon and Brent

TO-DO LIST
Ask for gift certificates

Gift certificates to your favorite maternity store make great gifts if you're on a tight clothing budget. You're bound to have an anniversary, birthday, or holiday during your pregnancy. So don't be shy; if someone asks you what you want, tell them that a gift certificate, even for a small amount, would be much appreciated. You can make a joke by saying, "Whoever gets me the biggest gift certificate gets the baby named after him or her. Ha, ha. Only kidding."

AT THIS POINT
You may be naming stuffed animals

Your friends and relatives will soon be purchasing all kinds of things for your baby—rattles, shirts, socks, and of course, stuffed animals. You'll know you have crossed into another dimension of your life when you start referring to your baby's future teddy bears as "Mr. Wiggles" or "Miss Fuzzy." (And you thought you weren't a natural!)

ADVICE FROM THE TRENCHES
Borrowing maternity clothes

"Maternity clothes are expensive, so borrow as much as you can. Women love to share their maternity clothes. Make sure you keep a list of who gave you what and who wants their maternity clothes back. You think you'll remember, but by the time you have your baby, you won't!"
—Betsy, mom to Hayden

day 196

TO-DO LIST

Jump up and down (gently) with excitement

You've waited and waited and finally, it's here. You're 12 weeks pregnant. If you haven't heard your baby's heartbeat yet, you will soon. You may still have morning sickness, fatigue, and a host of other symptoms, but hearing your baby's heartbeat will give you the emotional lift you need to get through the end of this often difficult trimester.

HOW TO VISUALIZE YOUR BABY

Think of a large lime—around 2¹/₂ inches (6.3 cm) long— with a strong heartbeat. She weighs nearly ¹/₂ ounce (14 g). The genitalia are starting to show some differentiation in sex, so within a week or so, you may start getting a boy or girl vibe. Her intestines, which developed within the umbilical cord, have now moved into her abdomen. Her kidneys have begun to produce and excrete urine, which she needs to help her stay afloat.

THE WHOLE TRUTH AND NOTHING BUT

Your baby is swimming in urine!

Yes, your baby floats in amniotic fluid, which is made by your placenta, and from your baby's own urine. (And you thought you were doing all the work!) This watery fluid is inside the amniotic membrane or sac and surrounds your baby throughout your pregnancy. Amniotic fluid cushions your baby from pokes, helps her develop her lungs by breathing and exhaling the fluid, lets her move around and build muscles, and maintains her temperature.

Right now, your baby's amniotic fluid level is just over 3 ounces (100 ml). Her fluid level will be at its greatest volume at around week 34, when it averages 27 ounces (800 ml). Your baby has a lot more peeing to do.

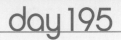
THE WHOLE TRUTH AND NOTHING BUT
You'll forget a lot of this later

It may be very hard for you to believe right now, but once you're in the throes of motherhood—especially new babyhood and then toddlerhood—you'll forget a lot of your pregnancy experience. That's why you should write down what you're feeling and experiencing. You don't have to keep a fancy journal. Just a plain notebook or even a personal online blog will do.

ADVICE FROM THE TRENCHES
Keep two journals

"I bought the nice hardcover journal with illustrations for my baby journal. This is where I recorded all of my happy thoughts. And then I bought a spiral-bound notebook, and that's where I vented and basically bitched about how sick I felt, my doubts about being a good mom, and all of the other hard things. Someday, if my daughter becomes pregnant, I will give her both. They are both important records of the best thing I ever did in my life."
—Wendy, mom to Shyanne

TO-DO LIST
Find another new mom for support

If you want to feel understood and supported, find a mom with a six- or eight-month old (so she's not overwhelmed with a newborn). She will be a great source of comfort and information. She will still remember what she went through and can "feel for you" on a level that makes you feel truly understood.

THE WHOLE TRUTH AND NOTHING BUT

What's happening with your breasts?

> **QUESTION:** Where are my big, gorgeous breasts?
>
> **ANSWER:** In your S.O.'s imagination, where they've always been.

By now, you may have noticed that your breasts are bigger. In Pregnancy Land, there is, of course, huge variation in what "bigger" means. Some women get a lot bigger—two or more cup sizes—and some women don't. But in general, your most rapid breast gain occurs in your first trimester, with a break in the second and a growth spurt again in the third. The average breast weight gain for most pregnant women is one to two pounds (450–950 g) and one to two cups sizes. (However, weighing them in the produce section of the grocery store, while understandably tempting, is strongly discouraged. They already think you're stealing ginger ale and crackers.)

But bigger in Pregnancy Land doesn't always mean better—especially when your breasts are still tender. Now, bigger when it comes to breasts means bluer, lumpier, and stretchier (as in stretch marks). This is cold comfort for small-breasted women who often hope to walk on that big-breasted wild side during pregnancy but don't get the huge big breasts they were counting on, yet still get lumpier ones. However, if you do get big breasts during pregnancy, don't get too attached—after pregnancy and breastfeeding, most women do return to their pre-pregnancy breast size.

As your breasts prepare for breastfeeding, they enlarge because of engorgement of blood vessels (read: those lovely bulging blue lines now under your skin) to promote blood flow to your breasts. After that, estrogen stimulates growth of the ducts, and progesterone stimulates growth of the glandular tissue (read: the lumps).

TO-DO LIST
Buy a bra extender

If your bra still fits cup-wise but feels tight across your back, an extender that hooks onto your hooks can buy you some more time in your current bra. That way you can wait and see how much your cup size goes up by the end of this trimester before buying a new bra. Bra extenders are cheap and are available at most maternity stores that sell bras and underwear.

AT THIS POINT
Maternity pants or transitional pants?

Living in one pair of velour sweat pants?

Seriously, you probably are in one pair of pants by now—two if you're lucky. But if maternity clothes are too huge right now, what can you do?

Transitional pants—in the next size up—work well for some women. Buying pants in the next size up may feel like a waste of money since you'll be out of them soon, plus they may be huge in the legs and the behind. But remember that not only will you wear them pre-maternity, you'll wear them postpartum as you're working your way down.

A solution for other women is to go with the trendy under-belly, low-rise maternity pants and jeans without panels. Some women love them for comfort and also for the hipness (which for years had been sorely missing in maternity fashion). Some prefer the new roll-paneled maternity pants that are designed especially for months 3 to 6. You roll the panel up and over your belly as necessary. And then you can wear them on the way back down.

ADVICE FROM THE TRENCHES
Roll it down

"Here is the best trick: If the front panel on your maternity jeans is too big right now, just roll the panel down for a better and comfier fit. If you're on a tight budget, this can save you from buying transitional pants or the three- to six-month roll panel pants that you will quickly outgrow."
—Sima, mom to Rohit

HOW TO STRETCH YOUR MATERNITY WARDROBE DOLLARS

* **Always buy solid colored skirts and pants in brown, black, or gray for flexibility.** Be colorful on top.

* **Hit the consignment stores.** These places are a gold mine of transitional and maternity clothes.

* **Check out eBay.** You can find great bargains on great maternity clothes.

* **Steal your S.O.'s favorite oxford shirt.** When it comes to hiding that new belly, a man's oxford shirt is a must right now. Why buy one when you can "borrow" one from the closet next to yours?

* **If you have to dress up for work, you can keep wearing your jackets.** Just keep them open and no one will know the difference.

With your new black pants, a colorful T-shirt under the oxford, sleeves stylishly rolled up, and your new consignment shop scarf, you'll look so good, you'll forget you're pregnant . . . for three seconds.

THE WHOLE TRUTH AND NOTHING BUT
Just how big will your uterus get?

If you feel like your uterus is already big and your pants are already tight, buckle your seatbelt.

Before you became pregnant, your uterus was practically solid—about the size of your fist and the shape of a pear. It weighed about 2½ ounces (71 g). During pregnancy, your uterus transforms into a round and thin-walled, muscular holder of baby, placenta, and amniotic fluid, increasing its capacity five hundred to one thousand times. By the end of your pregnancy, your uterus will weigh a whopping 2½ pounds (1.1 kg).

AT THIS POINT
Boy or girl?

If you could see into your uterus right now—at just about 13 weeks—you would be able to tell the sex of your baby. The external genitalia have now developed enough to distinguish between a boy or girl. Unfortunately, you can't see in there right now, so you'll just have to remain in suspense.

THE WHOLE TRUTH AND NOTHING BUT
Everyone has a guess

As soon as people find out you're pregnant, you'll start hearing the wives' tales, myths, and groundless predictions about the sex of your baby. Everyone you meet—from the clerk at the grocery store to your boss—has a theory about how to determine the sex based on heartbeats, needles on strings, and the shape of your protruding belly. None of it's true, but you might have fun guessing, anyway.

day 190

DOCTOR'S ORDERS
Do not do the Drano test

"In an effort to determine the sex of their baby, many women pursue various myths out there on how to predict the gender. Some are harmless, like twirling rings over your stomach, but some, such as the Drano test, aren't. Described on numerous Web sites, the Drano test requires you to mix your urine with chemicals that unclog drains; the color is then supposed to reveal the sex of your baby. The fumes and chemicals can be very dangerous, and this test has absolutely no basis in fact. Please don't do this! You'll find out the sex soon enough."
—K.N.

THE WHOLE TRUTH AND NOTHING BUT
Is taking a bath bad for baby?

Another old wives' tale debunked! Unless you bathe in extremely hot water, you have nothing to worry about. In general, you should avoid baths or hot tubs that raise your body temperature above 102 or 103 degrees Fahrenheit (39°C). So go ahead and pamper yourself with a warm bath.

TO-DO LIST
Buy some natural nail products

Speaking of pampering yourself . . . give yourself a manicure! Some women get beautiful, strong nails during pregnancy. Others find just the opposite, and their nails can become brittle or chipped. It's not fair, but pregnancy side effects never are.

If you want to do your nails—either to showcase them, or hide how badly they look—but don't want the chemicals or fumes right now, buy natural nail products and acetate-free remover (it takes a little more work than the toxic alternative, but it does work). Visit a natural foods supplier for more information.

HOW TO VISUALIZE YOUR BABY

Back in the pregnancy fruit bowl! Your baby is about the length of a lemon (3 inches or 7.6 cm), and he weighs about 3/4 ounce (19 g). If you need a break from the fruit bowl, think of a shrimp.

His eyes—currently on the sides of his head—will begin moving to the front. This is the start of your baby's face. By the end of this week, his ears will move to the proper spots. His tiny and unique fingerprints are now in place.

AT THIS POINT
You're in the final first trimester stretch

You're almost to your second trimester. So what if you haven't done the laundry in three weeks? So what if all you have in your refrigerator is condiments? You've got a heartbeat and one-third of your pregnancy under your belt (which is, of course, on the last possible notch).

TO-DO LIST
Give yourself an information-age break

It's wonderful to be in Pregnancy Land and to have so much advice and guidance available. Information can empower you, but if you get too much, you'll end up with a lot of things to worry about—and that's not good. So give yourself a periodic information blackout. As a matter of fact, close this book right now, turn off your computer, and take a nap.

day 188

DOCTOR'S ORDERS
Give yourself a reality check

"If you're really, really sick and vomiting every day and you're worried about your baby's health because nothing seems to stay down, call your doctor. But know that if you're able to choke down your prenatal vitamin, water, and some form of food, you and your baby are probably fine. At this point, your baby is still very tiny and his or her caloric needs are not great."
—K.N.

AT THIS POINT
Start your belly album

Chronicle the many stages of your changing belly. Choose one spot in your house to take belly shots so you'll have the same background each time. Then buy an inexpensive and pliable (soft covered) photo album that holds one photo per page. Take one shot a week, or as often as you'd like, and only put photos on the right side of the album. When you get to the end of your pregnancy, you can flip through the pages quickly to watch a little movie of your belly growing bigger. (Hey, when you're overdue and stuck in your house, you need all the fun you can get.)

Thanks to the queasies and vomiting you're experiencing on The Pregnancy Diet (the original yo-yo diet), you may actually be thinner now—but you still need a photo of it. Think of it as the "before" shot. Don't worry, the yo-yo will go up again in your next trimester and, in time, you'll look back on this first photo with great wistfulness.

ADVICE FROM THE TRENCHES
Well-meaning friends

"Your well-meaning, but not always helpful, friends without children will say things like, 'You worry too much' or 'Stress isn't good for the baby' (as if they had medical degrees or children at home). You have to remember they don't understand what you're going through. They think they know what pregnancy is like—but they don't. You probably thought you knew what pregnancy was going to be like, and now look at you!"
—Jenna, mom to Shane and Claire

AT THIS POINT
Be careful who you complain to

When people ask you, "How do you feel?" think carefully before blurting, "Sick and tired. I'm going to go insane if this nausea doesn't go away soon. This is so much harder than I thought it would be."

Though this may be true, by admitting it, you open yourself up to hearing about every crummy thing that person or his or her sister, friend, cousin, or hairdresser experienced—"Honey, that's nothing, my sister threw up for twenty-three weeks straight and had to be put on an IV."

THE WHOLE TRUTH AND NOTHING BUT
The fire in your chest

Speaking of complaining: Get those heartburn tablets ready. Heartburn often sets in by now and can ruin a perfectly good meal and nap. Hormones cause it, so modifying your diet won't always eliminate the problem. However, your favorite spicy food can definitely make it worse.

# day 186

AT THIS POINT
Are you tired of this science experiment?

You're probably wondering if there's any part of your body that will remain unchanged for the rest of your pregnancy, since most of your body seems profoundly changed—and you still have a long way to go.

Believe it or not, there *is* a part that won't change: your ears. Your ears will not be affected by your pregnancy. Ears don't swell, change color, expand, emit odors, release liquid, itch, fall off, or require any special attention, clothing, padding, worry, or fear.

Ears rule!

THE WHOLE TRUTH AND NOTHING BUT
Pregnancy takes forever

Yes, you're thrilled to almost be in your second trimester, but now it's hitting you: The most important event of your life is still 186 days away, and that's only if you deliver on your due date—which most women don't.

If the prospect of waiting 186 days or more to meet your baby seems like agony, be happy you're not a giraffe. Giraffes have a gestation of 425 days. If you and a giraffe got pregnant on the same day, by the time a giraffe gives birth you will have been back in normal underwear for nearly six months.

Be really, really happy you're not an elephant. These poor animals have a gestation period of 640 days. That means if you and an elephant got pregnant on the same day, your baby would be in preschool by the time she gave birth!

day 185

AT THIS POINT
You're all woman, you just sound like a man

Though being pregnant is the ultimate female experience, you probably don't feel very ladylike, especially since, thanks to your newly sluggish digestive system, gassiness in the form of copious burps and farts has set in. (Ducking behind bushes to pee doesn't help, either.) Look at it this way—for years, your S.O. has had no problem unleashing his bodily functions upon you.

HOW TO SEE YOUR S.O.'S POV RIGHT NOW

Meanwhile, even if he's super sensitive, your S.O. has absolutely no clue about what's going on in your body and why your emotions are irrational. Secretly, he will remember your former PMS episodes with fondness, craving the simplicity and predictability of your annoyance with him. If it will cheer you up, he probably won't mind you unleashing your bodily functions on him.

THE WHOLE TRUTH AND NOTHING BUT
There's no perfect in pregnancy

Here you are, burping and farting all over your S.O., barely cutting it at work, and your house is falling apart. You probably feel like a miserable, pregnant loser. You're not a loser, but don't try to be perfect—that will lead to disappointment. No matter how hard you try to do everything right, there will always be a better pregnant woman than you, and she's probably your sister, friend, or neighbor. Start trying not to be perfect right now. You have enough to do, like trying to find underwear that fits.

HOW TO KEEP FROM FEELING DOWN

When you feel sick and tired and don't look your best, it's hard to be upbeat. Don't make it worse by buying magazines featuring pregnant celebrities. You never see photographs of celebrities vomiting. You only see them buying $800 baby strollers and walking around in their $300 maternity shirts while real pregnant women are combing the aisles in Motherhood and Babies 'R Us looking for sales or telling people, "No, really, I'm not fat. I'm just pregnant."

THE WHOLE TRUTH AND NOTHING BUT
What will your second trimester be like?

A few weeks into your second trimester, most Pregnancy Land-ers start to feel (dare you believe?) better—a whole lot better. But you should also be prepared for the fact that while nausea and vomiting usually go away, there is a whole new set of aches and pains and symptoms that may arrive. Back aches, abdomen aches, leg cramps, constipation, and strange—though explainable—things, like moles and dark patches, may appear on your skin. But there is an undeniable bright side to the arrival of your second trimester: You're one-third of the way there.

AT THIS POINT
You may already be producing colostrum

Though your countdown day is still 184 days off, your breasts—regardless of their size—may have already started making colostrum. Colostrum, also called "pre-milk," is the nutrient- and antibody-rich fluid that feeds your baby and helps keep her healthy for the first few days after birth, before your milk comes in.

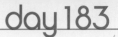

THE WHOLE TRUTH AND NOTHING BUT
There is no more "simple"

Accept it before it destroys you: There is no more simple in Pregnancy Land. Even something as innocent as drinking water (remember: eight to ten glasses a day) becomes a job during pregnancy. Even though you will start to feel better soon, there are still a hundred more unexpected symptoms waiting to unsimplify your life and your pregnancy.

TO-DO LIST
Find a special way to mark your first trimester's end

You did it; you survived what many women believe is the hardest trimester— although some argue that the third is the hardest. But even if it is, you still get a break in the second trimester.

Celebrate! If you're feeling better, it's time for a nice romantic dinner with your S.O. However, if you feel better but not that much better, skip the romance. Instead, take your calendar, rip off the months you've made it through, tear them up, throw them on the floor, and do a dance on them. You've earned it.

ADVICE FROM THE TRENCHES
The little things count

"To celebrate my first trimester's end, I went to the hardware store and bought a new toilet seat. I got sick of seeing the old one so up close and personal, every day, several times a day, for months straight."
—Dana, mom to Evan

THE SECOND
TRIMESTER

day 182

AT THIS POINT
You've made it to the second trimester!

Welcome to your honeymoon trimester—or what's called "the trimester that saved my relationship," "the only really good trimester you get," or "the trimester when my narcolepsy finally ended."

This is Pregnancy Land in all its glory. You'll get to see your baby with an ultrasound, you can find out the sex of the baby, you can have sex again—maybe even the best sex of your life! Energy returns, nausea stops, and you'll eat like a Viking after the plunder. Once your sickness has passed, the second trimester definitely has some perks.

ADVICE FROM THE TRENCHES
The second trimester delay

"You hear and read so much about the wonderful second trimester. When mine started, I still felt horrible, looked horrible, and I still wasn't showing. In my opinion, they should move the second trimester up a few weeks just so you're not disappointed when you hit week 14 and still feel like garbage."
—Renee, mom to Steven and Anderson

DOCTOR'S ORDERS
Pace yourself

"Though your first trimester is behind you, you still have a long road ahead. If you still don't feel well, hang on: Relief is coming, usually by the sixteenth week. And you may still be on the emotional roller coaster quite a bit. As far as life changes go, they still don't get much bigger than this."
—K.N.

day 181

HOW TO VISUALIZE YOUR BABY

At 14 weeks, your baby is about 3½ inches (8.9 cm) long from crown to rump, just a little longer than a lemon. He weighs about 1 ounce (28 grams). He's very thin-skinned (physically, not emotionally). By the end of this week, his arms will be in proportion to the rest of his body—though it's definitely too soon for a baseball glove, as his hands are still only about a half inch (1.3 cm) long.

By now, your baby has produced sweat glands, and his liver and pancreas are secreting fluids.

If you're having a girl, she now has about two million eggs in her ovaries, which will increase to about six million in another month, but this number will drop to a mere one or two million by the time she's born.

AT THIS POINT
What cool tricks can your baby do?

As your second trimester begins, your baby's little bag of tricks gets more interesting. She can now squint, frown, and grimace (all just reflexes right now, but they'll come in handy later, when she wants to eat cookies instead of broccoli). She can also grasp with her hands now.

And what cool tricks can you do? You can still get out of a chair without help, and you can still see your pubic hair without a mirror.

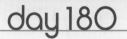
AT THIS POINT
Test decision time

Now for the second trimester downside: **TESTS**.

If you are under thirty-five years of age, you will be offered the "triple screen," a set of three hormonal blood levels that assess the risk of neural tube defects (spine abnormalities that can result in paralysis) or Down syndrome. This is done between weeks 16 and 22. If you are over thirty-five you will be offered an amniocentesis if you haven't had a CVS already. If you had a CVS you will just get the Alpha Fetoprotein (AFP) blood test, which will screen for neural tube defects.

Regardless of your age, whether to take the screening or not is a difficult decision to make and often comes down to personal beliefs. You and your S.O. should ask yourselves, what will we do with the information if we find out there's a problem?

DOCTOR'S ORDERS
Understand the purpose of every test

"The triple screen test doesn't definitively tell you whether your baby has a birth defect or Down syndrome—it just assesses the risk. If the test shows a higher risk than expected, then you will be offered an amniocentesis, which can definitively tell you. However, the triple screen has a false positive rate of 5 percent, meaning it says your risk is increased when truly your baby is normal. Many couples ask, 'Why not do an amniocentesis from the beginning?' The reason is that there is a one in two hundred chance of miscarrying a normal baby from the procedure itself."
—K.N.

day 179

HURRY UP AND WAIT ALERT
Where is the stomach already?

"Showing" is a major pregnancy milestone for all pregnant women. It kills you to feel so transformed emotionally and physically but not "stomachally." Although the top of your uterus, that fabulous fundus, is probably only just above your pelvic bone, it may be enough to push your stomach out a little, giving rise to the "bump," as it is often called. Many first-time moms don't really start to show until the twentieth week, the fifth month of pregnancy. It's hard to wait for this milestone—but before you know it, you're gonna pop.

ADVICE FROM THE TRENCHES
Showing, all right!

"I was showing before I even got pregnant, thanks to my first two pregnancies."
—Jennifer, mom of three beautiful children

TO-DO LIST
Start shopping for baby furniture now

Here's an unpleasant surprise—it can take up to twelve weeks to get delivery of baby furniture! If you're using the traditional baby store furniture route, you should start shopping now and order soon.

But don't panic if your crib and changing table won't arrive until after your due date. When you leave the hospital, all you really need is a car seat to get the baby home safely and some kind of bassinette for her to sleep in. You probably won't be using your baby's crib for the first few months, and all you need to change a baby is a changing pad or a blanket. Babies don't care, just the moms do.

day 178

THE WHOLE TRUTH AND NOTHING BUT
Baby furniture costs a fortune!

Here's an even more unpleasant baby furniture surprise—it can be really expensive. Unless you're getting hand-me-downs from generous relatives, you can expect to spend a lot of money. So if you know people with young children, start dropping hints now. Just make sure that if you get a used crib or mattress it meets the current safety standards. You can get guidelines from the U.S. National Safety Council and other safety organizations simply by searching online.

AT THIS POINT
Consider alternative furniture sources

If baby furniture cost is an issue (and it is for many), you may want to go the alternative route by buying separate pieces from various places that sell baby furniture but don't specialize in it. The other advantage to shopping outside the baby store circuit is you can often get delivery within a week or two.

ADVICE FROM THE TRENCHES
Go for the combo dresser/changing table

"I wish that I had just gotten the baby dresser with the changing table built right in. After my second baby arrived, she was in a much smaller room, and both pieces were hard to fit."
—Lucy, mom to Annabelle and Christina

HOW TO BE REALISTIC ABOUT YOUR WEIGHT GAIN

Do yourself a favor: Let go of whatever image you have in your head about exactly how much weight you'll gain and how you'll look by the end of your pregnancy.

Looking like Madonna or Cindy Crawford would be nice.

Forget it. Weight gain is another aspect of pregnancy that puts you under tons of pressure and that you don't have complete control over. Yes, you can control how much ice cream you're going to eat, but even an ideal weight gain boils down to genetics and body build.

DOCTOR'S ORDERS
Think in terms of average, not ideal, weight gain

"Each woman is unique, and each pregnancy is a little different, so rather than thinking of ideal weight, it's better to think of average weight gain—which, depending on your starting weight, will be from 25 to 35 pounds (11–15 kg). It's true that studies have shown that excessive weight gain can carry increased risks, particularly in women who are already overweight, but if you weren't overweight at the beginning of your pregnancy, some women can still maintain good health at 40-plus pounds (18 kg).

"I was one of those women! Though I ate balanced meals, I found I couldn't always beat the French fry cravings in my second trimester. So strive for balance, but if your doctor says you're healthy, don't obsess about your weight gain or overanalyze every morsel you place in your mouth."

—K.N.

THE WHOLE TRUTH AND NOTHING BUT
Your appetite will scare you (and others)

A big appetite in pregnancy is not like a big appetite in non-pregnancy. It's not a "maybe I'll have an apple and a cookie now" kind of hunger. It's more like, "I'll eat this half a watermelon, the entire roast chicken for dinner, and this pie looks good. What are you going to eat, hon?"

HOW TO KISS THE SOUTH BEACH DIET GOODBYE IN FOUR SIMPLE STEPS

Your need for more carbs will become quite evident during your second trimester. If you were on a carb-restricted eating plan before you became pregnant, you may need to do the following:

1. Pick up a box of Double Stuf Oreos.

2. Do not read the carb content.

3. Eat two—okay three—before you even get to the cash register.

4. Remind yourself that while pregnancy has its downsides, eating more carbs is not one of them.

AT THIS POINT
You're revising your family plan (again)

Now that you're feeling better—in fact, a lot better—you're thinking you could do this another two times, maybe even three. This pregnancy business is not so bad. Yes, four children seems doable.

day 175

AT THIS POINT
What's happening in the fruit bowl?

At week 15 of life on the inside, your baby is now around 4 inches long (10 cm)—about the length of a pear—and weighs about 1 3/4 ounces (50 grams)—about as heavy as a grapefruit. Her legs are now longer than her arms, and she can move all of her joints and limbs. Get ready for a cute attack: Her eyebrows are beginning to grow, and the hair on her head may be sprouting.

HURRY UP AND WAIT ALERT
The not-so-quickening

You're just dying to feel the "quickening"—that's the term for feeling your baby move. Hang in there, that milestone is coming soon (within the next three to four weeks). In the meantime, think of it as the "not-so-quickening."

HOW TO ENTERTAIN YOURSELF WHILE WAITING

Play flashlight tag with your baby. Though your baby's eyelids are fused shut, her retinas can detect a small amount of light filtering through your tissue when you're in bright light. If you shine a flashlight at your belly, she's likely to move away from the beam. Though you can't feel it, it's still fun to think that she's moving around. However, just once is enough: You don't want your baby to be on the run in utero.

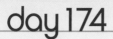
THE WHOLE TRUTH AND NOTHING BUT
Who was that masked man/woman?

It was your doctor whooshing in and whooshing out again! Every Pregnancy Land-er would love to have one hour—okay, five—with their doctor. But if he or she is part of a busy or large practice, you're probably only getting ten to fifteen minutes of face time per visit.

You may want to switch to a doctor who can give you more time, but the reality is that most doctors can spend only ten to fifteen minutes with you. Rather than complain or feel disappointed, accept the reality and be prepared.

Also: Remember to take full advantage of the nurse, nurse practitioner, and/or midwife, because people in these roles usually have more time to answer questions and address your fears.

DOCTOR'S ORDERS
Make the most of your time with your doctor

"Due to the high volume of most obstetrical practices, doctors are rushed for time, so it is important to get the most out of your visit. One way to accomplish this is to come prepared with a list of questions relevant to where you are in your pregnancy. If you aren't in your third trimester, you don't need to go over every detail of your birth plan. The good thing about prenatal visits is that you will have more than ten visits over your entire pregnancy, which provides you many opportunities to ask your questions."
—K.N.

day 173

TO-DO LIST
Buy a spiral notebook

If you wrote all of your questions on Post-It notes and attached them to your body, you would look like a pregnant chicken. Instead, buy a small notebook to write down all of your questions in one organized place. Before your appointments, review your list and choose your most important questions. But don't forget to take your notebook with you!

ADVICE FROM THE TRENCHES
Work with your doctor

"I found that if I told my doctor, 'I have three questions I really need answers to today,' I didn't feel rushed, and I always got the answers."
—Bonnie, mom to Morgan

DOCTOR'S ORDERS
Before you switch practices . . .

"It is very important to feel comfortable and cared for by your doctor. If the fit isn't right, by all means change. Just try to have reasonable expectations. If you have a million questions, ask yourself whether there is something underlying those questions, such as the intense fear of everything going wrong. Some of the scariest aspects of being pregnant are the lack of control and the fear of the unknown. If you can, describe your fears to your doctor. When you do this you are putting it right out there where your doctor can't miss it, and you can feel better by just saying it. Doctors have an easier time addressing your specific fears than answering a litany of questions."
—K.N.

AT THIS POINT
Frustrated with the system?

If you're finding it difficult to communicate with your doctor, or you're being worn out by tests and pregnancy technology, you have to remind yourself that you are living in an amazing and enlightened medical age, even though it doesn't always feel that way.

Here's how *Dunglison's Medical Dictionary* defined pregnancy circa 1850: "The state of a female who has within her ovary or womb a fecundated germ which gradually becomes developed in the latter receptacle."

Sounds more like you're putting out a recycling bin than having a baby! But at least the 1800s were a civilized time to have a baby. Pregnancy even made it into *Bouvier's Law Dictionary*, which contained this entry: "26-2. As to the duration of pregnancy. Lord Coke lays down the peremptory rule that 40 weeks is the longest time allowed by law for gestation."

Now that's a law we can all live with. Thank you, Lord Coke.

ADVICE FROM THE TRENCHES
Telling it like it is

"My doctor told me, 'Pregnancy is not an excuse for eating too much.' I said, 'I agree. It's not an excuse. It's the reason.'"
—Kate, mom to Julia and Ellie

# day 171

TO-DO LIST
Start checking out daycare now

Seriously. Now. Many daycares have waiting lists! So if you're considering daycare as an option, you need to start making calls and conducting interviews.

Seek out accredited childcare facilities; the Internet is a useful resource for finding potential facilities and getting helpful information on choosing a facility, what to look for, and what questions to ask. Your friends, coworkers, and neighbors who are working moms are another great resource for finding good quality daycare.

ADVICE FROM THE TRENCHES
Get dad on the job

"When you're pregnant, the last thing you want to be doing is schlepping around interviewing people to take care of the baby you don't even have yet. This is where your husband can totally come to the rescue and do some of the heavy lifting for you. Mine researched the options, put together a list of questions, asked them, and made the follow-up calls. He really took the burden off of me."
—Beth, mom to Jacob and Mitchell

THE WHOLE TRUTH AND NOTHING BUT
How much???

Another bummer: Daycare is expensive. The sooner you know what the cost will be, the sooner you can begin budgeting or exploring other options, like care in a home setting (this is a person who watches children in his or her own home) or begging your mother or mother-in-law to babysit two days a week for you. Start sucking up now.

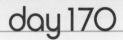

AT THIS POINT
Maternity leave conundrum

Here you are, making decisions about your maternity leave long before your baby is born. Except how do you know how much time you'll really want to have off, how your finances will shake out, and how you'll feel about going back to work?

A great book on the subject is *The Best Friend's Guide to Maternity Leave* by Betty Holcomb. Holcomb advises moms-to-be to ask for as much time as you can get without jeopardizing your job or going broke. She writes: "One of the most consistent things I've heard from the women I've interviewed over the years is that they wished they had asked for more time. . . . For most companies, twelve weeks of maternity leave is standard, but I personally feel it's best to try for four to six months, if possible. That's enough time to recuperate, enjoy the baby, and even get a little bored and ready to do some work at home. Remember, you can always ask for less time after the baby has arrived."

Good point.

ADVICE FROM THE TRENCHES
Don't be afraid to ask for what you want

"Don't be afraid to ask your boss for a more flexible work schedule. I work one day at home now, and it wouldn't have happened if I hadn't asked. All they can do is say no, but they might say yes."
—Vanessa, mom to Harry and one on the way

day 169

HURRY UP AND WAIT ALERT
Boy or girl?

Is the suspense driving you to distraction? If you have an ultrasound this week, you may be able to find out whether your baby is a boy or girl (his or her genitalia may be visible). But an ultrasound at 16 to 18 weeks will be more reliable at revealing sex.

DOCTOR'S ORDERS
Consider the surprise factor

"I tell my patients, 'There are very few surprises left in life, and if you can stand it, you should let yourself be surprised about the sex of your baby.' If you can't stand the suspense, most of the time the ultrasound will reveal the sex. But even then, you never know! There have been many times the nursery themes had to be changed after delivery! Amniocentesis and chorionic villi sampling are the only accurate tests that detect the sex."
—K.N.

THE WHOLE TRUTH AND NOTHING BUT
Give her some air!

By now, you may be noticing that you're huffing and puffing at the top of your stairs. Your lungs are really working it. Since your baby takes up more room now, there is less room for your lungs to expand. Pregnant women have to breathe faster to compensate for this change as well as to meet the increased oxygen demands of the fetus and mother. On top of all that, progesterone gives you the unpleasant sensation that you aren't getting enough air. But don't worry, you are.

day 168

HOW TO VISUALIZE YOUR BABY

In terms of his weight and length, think of a large avocado. He's about 4½ inches (11 cm) long (head to bottom) and weighs just under 3 ounces (85 grams). He's still very little, but his head is more erect and his body is longer than his head. Here's a cute little detail: His toenails are starting to grow. Need more cuteness? His nose is now fully formed and ready for tweaking.

TO-DO LIST
Make yourself some guacamole

If the mention of avocado has you craving guacamole, go for it. Avocado is loaded with heart-healthy fat, B vitamins, and fiber and keeps you nice and full for a long time. You don't even have to make guacamole, especially if the lime or garlic might aggravate your heartburn. Just take an avocado, mash it in a bowl, and spread it on whole grain blue corn chips or whole grain crackers.

AT THIS POINT
Your baby has taste buds, too

If you're eating spicy foods now, your baby just may grow up liking foods such as guacamole or peppers. By this week your baby's taste buds already look like a mature adult's, and amniotic fluid can smell strongly of garlic and spices from the mother's diet. (Maybe you should start eating broccoli every day, just to set a good example.)

day 167

TO-DO LIST
Reintroduce yourself to your S.O.

Hello, you're awake! Look up from your puddle of drool and tell your S.O.: "Hi, honey, I've missed you too!" Now don't waste another minute. Go to the movies.

AT THIS POINT
You may have your "mojo" back

On the hottie mom scale, you're not just out of the negative; you may just break a 10. Finally! Something positive comes from all those hormones and the increased blood volume coursing through your body—there's a lot of it flowing through your genitals now and that means *great sex*. The hormones, increased blood to your genitals, plus the absence of first trimester narcolepsy can add up to an increased desire for sex. Some women also have more intense orgasms that are easier to achieve.

THE WHOLE TRUTH AND NOTHING BUT
But my baby is in there!

Now for the other side of the "mojo" coin. Though you will hear a lot about the great sex during pregnancy, this doesn't mean you will always have it. Complications may ensue—like the fact that you will both be a little unsettled by knowing that there is a baby "in there." You may feel somewhat self-conscious if you've suddenly become the initiator in the relationship. (Don't worry, your S.O. probably won't complain.) Remember, pregnancy is a time of extremes—and this goes for sex drive too. When it's on, it's on, and when it's off, no amount of dynamite can blast it open.

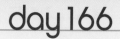

THE WHOLE TRUTH AND NOTHING BUT
Your S.O. may be afraid to have sex

Here's what every man on the entire planet wants to know about having sex with his pregnant partner:

"During sex, can my baby feel my penis?"

DOCTOR'S ORDERS
Sex is safe

"There are only a few situations where sex is not allowed in pregnancy. If your doctor hasn't put a ban on sex, then you are free to explore the benefits of sex during pregnancy. Don't worry, the baby is well cushioned in her amniotic fluid. Don't be surprised if you have mild contractions during orgasm. As long as they stop and don't intensify, it's normal. Think of it as an aftershock."
—K.N.

ADVICE FROM THE TRENCHES
You did it before and look what happened!

"Sometimes, hormones or not, you just don't feel like having sex. It is, after all, what got you to this point in the first place!"
—Jen, mom to Jack and Madison

ADVICE FROM THE TRENCHES
Bring it on!

> *"I was expecting to get my libido back in my second trimester. Imagine my surprise at getting Samantha's from* Sex and the City *instead!"*
> —Anonymous mother

AT THIS POINT
You may have to take matters into your own hands

Yes, let's blush for a moment, but masturbation during pregnancy is perfectly safe—with or without standard devices—and it's a great pastime while you're counting down. If you don't have tons of experience in this area, watch *Sex and the City* reruns for inspiration.

TO-DO LIST
Start exercising

If you're awake enough to have sex and you're not vomiting anymore, it's time to hit the gym or great outdoors. Exercise can help you sleep better, boost your energy, and cut stress. Walking, yoga, swimming, stationary biking, and using an elliptical machine are great low-impact exercise choices, especially if you've never exercised regularly before. Take it slow and build your strength up.

DOCTOR'S ORDERS
Adjust your workouts

> *"If you were active pre-pregnancy, you can continue your usual routine as long as you make some adjustments as you go along. Make sure you are not at risk for injuring your belly by falling or by getting a blow or kick. You need to avoid lying flat on your back when you pass 20 weeks.* Fit Pregnancy *is a great magazine that can help you adjust your workouts. I highly recommend it."*
> —K.N.

AT THIS POINT
You've probably heard about . . .

. . . the pregnant woman who ran a marathon. Seriously. Sue Olden from Burnsville, Minnesota, ran a marathon in 4 hours and 50 seconds—while 8 months pregnant.

. . . your decreased ability to burn fat through exercise. This is true, too—it appears that the hormonal changes found in pregnancy override your body's ability to burn fat through exercise. Conclusion: You need fat in pregnancy. (Take comfort wherever you can get it!)

. . . a very pregnant Olympic athlete. Germany's Cornelia Pfohl competed in Athens in 2004 even though she was 30 weeks pregnant. She is believed to be the first woman to compete in the Olympics during her third trimester. Thankfully, she competed in archery and not gymnastics.

DOCTOR'S ORDERS
Know the new exercise guidelines

"The old guidelines for exercising in pregnancy said women should not allow their heart rates to go above 140 beats per minute. This wasn't very scientific and didn't account for variations in normal healthy women. The best guideline is making sure you can have a full conversation at the peak of exercise. If you can't speak normally, then you are doing too much. It is also important to keep yourself hydrated throughout."
—K.N.

ADVICE FROM THE TRENCHES
Exercise while you can

"Exercise while you can. You never know when a weird pregnancy symptom might bench you. I got painful feet in my fourth month and was disappointed to have to stop even walking."
—Lisa, mom to Jake and Ally

 # day 163

AT THIS POINT
Exercisus interruptus

If you're a frequent urinator, you may find it really difficult to even go for a brisk twenty-minute walk without needing to stop. If you don't feel comfortable on the treadmill in a gym (you may be afraid of falling or just uncomfortable in the gym now), here are some ideas for you:

* Hit the mall and do laps (this is a great place to walk when the weather is too hot or too cold). And, of course, you can get a snack if you need it and shop afterward.

* Circle your block and stop in your house when you need it. So what if your neighbors are saying things like, "Here she comes again!"

* Find a park with a walking/running track and a restroom—but make sure the restroom is actually open, working, and has no creepy people lurking around. (Avoid paved recreation areas that are too crowded or have rollerbladers and bikers. You don't want to risk getting bumped or hit.)

ADVICE FROM THE TRENCHES
Even Olympic moms have challenges

"A lot of women say they love being pregnant, but I wasn't such a big fan. As an athlete who's used to being in peak form, it was challenging for me to watch my body totally change, since I had no control over that. I loved having my baby inside of me, but I was very happy when he was finally here."
—Marion Jones, Olympic gold medalist and mother of two

THE WHOLE TRUTH AND NOTHING BUT

Does exercise really make labor easier?

You read this in just about every book and Web site known to pregnant women. But is a shorter, easier labor really in your future if you exercise?

Yes, and there are a lot of official studies to back up the claim. In 1996, *The American Journal of Sports Medicine* reported that women who exercised got out of Pregnancy Land an average of five days earlier than others—with less medical intervention (such as induction and episiotomies). The study also found that women who exercised had a shorter "active phase" (read: the really painful part) by two hours.

In 1991, *The American Journal of Obstetrics and Gynecology* reported that women who continued running or aerobic dancing during pregnancy enjoyed 30 percent shorter labors than women who didn't exercise.

DOCTOR'S ORDERS

Think of labor as a marathon

"Since the energy you expend during labor is close to that of running a marathon, the stronger your muscles are and the greater your endurance is the more likely you will be able to go the distance. Pushing can sometimes take three hours, especially if you have an epidural. You can imagine how hard it is to sustain that intensity. The exercise you do doesn't have to be intense. Prenatal yoga and walking are two great forms of exercise you can start even for the first time in pregnancy. Yoga helps you prepare physically and mentally for delivery."
—K.N.

day 161

HOW TO VISUALIZE YOUR BABY

Spread your hand open wide. Study the distance from the top of your thumb to the bottom of your palm. At 17 weeks of pregnancy, this is the size of your baby—about 5 inches (12.7 cm). Your baby weighs about 6 ounces (170 grams). The cartilage of her skeleton is hardening to bone. Fat is just now forming under her skin. The bones of her ears and the nerve endings from her brain are now, or will soon be, developed enough for her to hear your voice and your heartbeat. So you can start saying, "I love you," and maybe she'll hear you and raise her eyebrows—because she's got those now, too.

TO-DO LIST
Play music near your growing belly

Now that your baby's sense of hearing is developing, it's time to start introducing her to your favorite music. While there are no studies that indicate that music makes any difference in fetal development, it's still fun to think your baby can hear the music you like. Don't get suckered into buying classical music if you're not already a fan. Why play music in utero that your child will never hear again in your house or car?

THE WHOLE TRUTH AND NOTHING BUT
Can you only gain tummy weight?

If you could, do you think you would see pregnant women with big butts ever again? It's hard not to get big all over when you're growing another person. Try not to obsess if your butt gets big. What goes up does come down (in time).

day 160
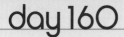

AT THIS POINT
Your ultrasound is going to happen soon

It's almost here—the moment you've been waiting for. You finally get to see your baby! And some of you will even get to see your babies, because that's the biggest surprise an ultrasound can deliver—the news that you're having twins, triplets, or more. If you want to find out the sex of your baby, the ultrasound will probably reveal this much-coveted news.

DOCTOR'S ORDERS
Leave siblings at home

"Many moms-to-be imagine this wonderful image where they are with their partner and other children sharing in the ultrasound, seeing the baby for the first time. While most of the time it is a wonderful experience, there can be some unexpected news. If there is some complication that needs to be addressed, you are going to want to be able to focus on the doctor and not have to worry about your other children at that moment."
—K.N.

ADVICE FROM THE TRENCHES
Premonitions are sometimes just anxiety

"Because of a previous loss, I was so nervous about my ultrasound. Even though I had the triple screens done and they came back fine, and the heartbeat was nice and strong, I kept getting this nagging feeling that something was wrong. It felt like a premonition, I was so worried. I just kept thinking, 'I hope they find a healthy baby in there.' Happily, they did! So sometimes those nagging feelings are just plain old worry, not premonitions."
—A. J., mom to Catherine and Dixon

HOW TO MENTALLY PREPARE FOR YOUR ULTRASOUND

Not to take the wind out of your pregnancy sails, but an ultrasound is a medical procedure. Happily, it's a medical procedure with no pain and only minimal goo (from a cold gel that is put on your tummy so the handheld probe can move back and forth). But remember, it's still a procedure.

You may just want to see your baby (*finally*) but the technician or doctor doing the ultrasound will want to make sure everything about your baby's anatomy is normal and healthy. They do a lot of measuring—in silence—which will infuriate you. They will push buttons and adjust knobs like they're landing an airplane. Don't panic. They're just checking very carefully, and that's a good thing.

DOCTOR'S ORDERS
What an ultrasound really tells us

"Ultrasound tells us about the anatomy of your baby. It lets us see the different structures in the brain and in the heart. We can also evaluate the fluid around the baby to make sure there is an adequate amount. The position of the placenta and how it looks will be noted. When a series of ultrasounds are done in high-risk pregnancies, the growth of the baby can be assessed. Though ultrasound provides a lot of important information, you need to understand that an ultrasound can't definitively determine if there is a chromosomal or other abnormality invisible to the eye."
—K.N.

day 158

THE WHOLE TRUTH AND NOTHING BUT
What's that?

During the ultrasound, don't be embarrassed if you think you're looking at your baby's head, only to discover it's her bottom. Don't be shy about asking the technician for a complete explanation of what you're seeing and which body parts are which on your pictures, so that you can explain it to others later.

AT THIS POINT
You've got a mover and shaker on board

Once you are able to decipher what you are looking at on the ultrasound screen, you will be amazed by how much movement is going on without you feeling it. Because the baby is so little and there is so much fluid, the majority of her movements aren't felt. It is a magical moment to watch your baby's own special water ballet.

HOW TO LOOK AT THE ULTRASOUND PICTURES WITHOUT PANICKING

Be prepared for the fact the photographs you get from ultrasounds are not comparable to a Kodak moment. Your baby will not look like a baby. She will look like a funny little creature with big moon eyes and an "alien" head, or even worse, your Uncle Ed. The ultrasound is not an indication of what the baby will look like when she arrives. (Unless, of course, it's a cute picture. Then it counts.)

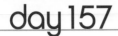

ADVICE FROM THE TRENCHE/
Ultrascared

> *"Don't expect your technician to announce, 'What a healthy looking baby—I rarely see them so well-formed!' You might hear, 'I don't see any abnormalities,' and you're thinking, 'Gee, thanks!'"*
> —Dana, mom to Evan

AT THI/ POINT
You want to know/don't want to know the sex

If you don't want to know the sex, the sex will be immediately and vividly apparent to the person doing your ultrasound, who will gleefully withhold the information. If you want to know, the baby will be sitting with his or her legs crossed. But be stubborn. Don't leave. Drink cold juice. Get up and move around. Poke your stomach. Sing loudly. Get that baby to uncross!

THE WHOLE TRUTH AND NOTHING BUT
You may have to pee badly

Depending on when exactly you have your ultrasound, you may not be required to drink a lot of water beforehand. The later you are, after week 17, the more the amniotic fluid serves to float your baby so you won't need a full bladder.

Unfortunately, if a full bladder during your ultrasound is necessary in order to get a good look, it can really put a damper on the whole experience. There's your baby on the screen, and of course you're thrilled, but you're also thinking, "I'm going to pee myself!"

TO-DO LIST
Play the sex game

No, not that game. This is the innocent "sex of the baby" game, and it's so easy and so much fun. If you're on the fence about whether to find out your baby's sex, bring a piece of paper and an envelope with you to your ultrasound appointment. Have the technician write the sex on a piece of paper and seal it up. Now, make a bet with your S.O. about who can hold out the longest without tearing it open.

ADVICE FROM THE TRENCHES
Get ready for angry friends and relatives

"If you decide, as we did, not to reveal your baby's sex, you will suddenly become unpopular with your family and friends. People will try to pry it out of you or will be hurt that you don't want to share the secret with them. My mother was mad for weeks. My advice? Stick to your guns; they'll get over it once the baby arrives. You can always claim that you don't know the sex to avoid the whole controversy."
—Anna, mom to Katie

HOW TO KEEP FROM FINDING OUT THE SEX OF YOUR BABY

Every time you walk into a doctor's office or an ultrasound room, hold up a sign with big letters that says: "I don't want to know the sex." You'd be surprised at the number of slip-ups that are made by well-meaning medical people.

day 155

TO-DO LIST
Start your first baby album

You now have your first picture for your baby's album. If you post your ultrasound picture on the refrigerator, make sure you put it in plastic for protection.

HOW TO CALM YOUR S.O.

The ultrasound is a big deal for you. But for your S.O., it's a huge moment when your pregnancy takes on new reality. You're in your body, which has been expanding, expelling, and itching ever since you missed your period. But for your S.O., actually seeing the baby can be nothing short of a mind-blowing experience. He may react with full-blown panic as well as joyful hysteria. Give him permission to panic and walk around in circles for several hours.

THE WHOLE TRUTH AND NOTHING BUT
"I was so sure it was a boy!"

Having a healthy child is the most important thing in the world—period. But if we're all being honest, some of us would have to admit that we were hoping for a girl or just felt like we were going to have a boy. Surprise, surprise—now you may know the opposite is true. Allow yourself to be surprised, disappointed, scared, or just unsure of how you're going to raise a boy, when you always saw yourself as a girl mom, or vice versa. And don't worry—all of your doubts and disappointment will go flying out the door the second you lay eyes upon your newborn, no matter what sex.

day 154

HOW TO VISUALIZE YOUR BABY

Your baby is about 5 1/2 inches (14 cm) long, or about the length of a large baking potato. He weighs almost 7 ounces (198 g). He's busy doing his aerobic workout with some very impressive kicks that you will feel any day now. If your baby is a boy, his penis and scrotum are visible. If your baby is a girl, her uterus and her fallopian tubes are now formed. Her vocal cords are developed, but without air, she can't test them out.

AT THIS POINT
You're the fruit!

Your uterus is the size of a big cantaloupe, and it probably feels that way, too. If you place your fingers below your bellybutton, you can no doubt feel it. By now, you may have gained around 10 to 14 pounds (4.5–6.4 kg). Expect to gain an average of about 1 pound (450 g) per week.

TO-DO LIST
Drink a big glass of cold orange juice

This is an exciting week for Pregnancy Land-ers. During their first pregnancies, many women feel their babies move for the first time right around now. If you haven't felt anything yet, drink a glass of cold orange juice—both the coldness and the sugar are known to get babies kicking—and lie down. Give your heart a chance to slow down. Breathe deeply and relax. Feel any butterflies? How about gas bubbles? You may not be nervous or gaseous—that fluttering and bubbling could be your baby on the move!

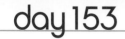# day 153

HURRY UP AND WAIT ALERT
No one else can feel movement yet

When you feel your baby move, it is a spectacular pregnancy moment. Unfortunately, it's going to take another few weeks before your partner gets to feel the baby move, too. Let him put his hand on your belly anyway, just in case.

ADVICE FROM THE TRENCHES
I felt something move

"There really isn't anything that compares to feeling your baby move for the first time. For me, it was the moment that my fetus became *my baby. I realized that we were sharing our own special world, and that world was my body."*
—Helene, mom to Cory

THE WHOLE TRUTH AND NOTHING BUT
Now you want more movement!

You wait and wait to feel your baby move. Then out of the blue: Bam! It happens. You get a flutter, pop, or kick. What a high! And then nothing for hours, even days! *Crash!*

You're not a negative person if you're tormenting yourself because your baby isn't moving enough. Every Pregnancy Land resident experiences this. But rest assured, as your baby grows, you will discover that you can tune in to your baby's wake and sleep cycles. By your third trimester you will have days that make you feel like you have a jumping bean on board, and you'll be exhausted by your baby's movement. For now, feeling your baby's movements is hit or miss.

AT THIS POINT
You're becoming a public figure

The bigger you get, the more you'll become a public figure. You may love the extra attention—at least until the end of your third trimester, at which point you'll growl at anyone who even looks at you. You might not enjoy the extra attention. If that's the case, you need to prepare yourself for the fact that everyone loves pregnant women. But console yourself with the fact that once you have the baby, nobody looks at you anymore—so try to enjoy the attention now.

ADVICE FROM THE TRENCHES
People say dumb/inconsiderate/insane things

"When I was still at the beginning of my second trimester, a woman at a party actually told me a story of a woman who had a bad experience during her second trimester. I'm not going to repeat the story—because then I'll be the person telling you something horrible. I'll just tell you that all's well that ends well. Mom and baby ended up just fine. But what the hell was this woman thinking?"
—Lucy, mom to Anabelle and Christina

THE WHOLE TRUTH AND NOTHING BUT
You can say, "I don't want to hear that!"

You're entitled not to hear horrible stories, especially any that involve pregnant women, babies, and dogs. Be prepared: You will become a magnet for them. Have a line prepared ahead of time. Interrupt and say, "Excuse me, but I'd rather not hear any more. I'm sure you understand why I find that kind of thing upsetting." Try to do it without calling the person an idiot, if you can.

# day 151

NOT-TO-DO LIST
The worst television to watch while you're pregnant

Law & Order and all of its derivatives (especially *Special Victims Unit*).

CSI and all of its derivatives. In fact, you might skip crime shows in general.

All-news channels. If the bad news doesn't make you seasick, the "crawl" on the bottom of the screen definitely will.

Oprah. The celebrity makeover shows are fun, safe bets. But skip the emotionally charged episodes about survival stories, medical miracles, and world hunger.

Judging Amy. It's all about kids getting screwed up—first by their parents and then by the judicial system.

The Baby Show. At least for now. The women in this show are ready to give birth. You're still recovering from ultrasound excitement.

MTV. Why worry about your baby as a teenager for another thirteen years?

Reality TV. Too much reality TV is not good for those in Pregnancy Land, especially if it involves bug eating!

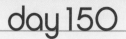

HOW TO THINK OF NAMES NO ONE ELSE HAS

Now that you know the sex of your baby, the Name Game takes on greater meaning and urgency and becomes a constant Pregnancy Land pastime. You really want to find the perfect name for your baby. Some parents want to be original, but thanks to soap operas, coming up with original baby names is tough stuff, though certainly not impossible. Here are some ideas you may not have thought of yet:

Condiments and Spices: A-1, Dijon, Soya, Cayenne, Bay, Tarragon, Cumin

Automobiles: Durango, Dodge, Honda, Toyota, Mercedes

Famous Brands: Tab, Pentium, Dell, Hewlett

Lesser-Used Months: January, March, November, September, October

Personality Traits and Talents: Gracious, Winner, Dancer, Archer

Geography: Bahama, France, India, Peru, Jamaica

TO-DO LIST
Perform the nickname test

Before you make your final baby name decision, you need to perform the nickname test. Take the name Richard: Do you really want your son being called "Dick?" You can just imagine the nicknames for "Regina" and "Virginia."

AT THIS POINT
Put your baby name in the vault

Once you decide on a name, don't reveal it to anyone. Here's why:

* Someone will say something bad about your name—like they knew a bully named Andrew or the biggest slut in their high school was named Avery.

* Someone might claim: "But that's the name I'm planning on using."

* It's fun to have some secrets.

HOW TO THINK OF TWO NAMES

If you're having twins, you may have an even harder time coming up with two great names. Here are three ideas:

* **Use anagrams.** The names Amy and May use the exact same letters in different order. So do Christina and Christian.

* **Different name, same meaning:** Get a book of meanings—You could find two names that mean the same thing in different languages. For example, Eve and Zoe both mean *life*, in Hebrew and Greek.

* **Reverse first name with middle name:** You can have a Paul Thomas and a Thomas Paul.

TO-DO LIST
Check out the Web

In the United States, the Social Security Administration provides the "official" list of the most popular names for boys—Jacob, Michael, and Joshua—and girls—Emily, Emma, Madison. (Other Web sites featuring popular names will rank them according to current popularity.) Plus, you can find out how a name you're considering has weathered in popularity over the years, the most popular names where you live, and the most popular names in other centuries.

day 148

AT THIS POINT
Keep the Name Game civil

Some couples have been known to argue for weeks about the baby's name. If you're having a hard time playing the Name Game with your S.O., here are the rules of fair play:

1. If it's been preordained that should this child be a male child *he must* carry your husband's hopefully not too geeky name choice, you automatically get to pick the name if it's a girl.

2. If your S.O. has a geeky name choice or a name that is the same as your creepy first roommate from college, try to compromise on the nickname. For example, Bartholomew could easily be Tom or Max, don't you think?

3. Celebrity names are a great place to start the Name Game as long as neither of you harbors a sexual fantasy about the actual person. But avoid the baby names celebrities are picking for their own children—you'll get tired of hearing, "Did you name her Apple after Gwyneth Paltrow's baby?"

4. No claiming that you had a dream in which you were told what the baby's name should be unless you really did dream it.

5. Above all, be mature and remember: Scissors cuts paper, rock smashes scissors, and paper covers rock.

day 147

HURRY UP AND WAIT ALERT
The halfway point!

Wow, you're almost there! Next week is your halfway point, a big countdown milestone. You're clearly showing, but you're not ultra huge. Start planning now for a fun way for you and your S.O. to celebrate your midpoint. You could do something that you won't get to do a lot once the baby arrives, like actually sitting down while eating.

HOW TO VISUALIZE YOUR BABY

Your baby weighs about 8 ounces (226 g). She measures approximately 6 inches (15 cm) long, about the length of a slice of watermelon. Her baby brain is busy developing millions of motor neurons. Once she's born, her brain will continue its rapid and dramatic development, just no longer on this microscopic level. She spends about six hours a day awake and eighteen or so asleep. This is (if you're lucky) the same schedule kept by a newborn.

THE WHOLE TRUTH AND NOTHING BUT
Growing pains (literally)

When you found out you were pregnant, you probably thought about the big-bang-like pain of delivery. That would be the "Honey, I think this is it!" moment. What you didn't imagine is how many aches and pains you'll have that are (here's that pesky pregnancy word again) *normal*.

If you think of how relaxed your joints are or how stretched your uterus is, you will realize all the work your body is doing to keep everything going. With this work come the aches in your abdomen, groin, and back. And as you get bigger, you may find that you get shooting pains down your legs, too.

DOCTOR'S ORDERS
Getting around round ligament pain

"You may notice a quick, stabbing pain on one or both of your sides. It's nothing to be alarmed about. This is called round ligament pain. Sometimes it can be quite intense and catch you when you bend or twist too quickly. The round ligaments go from the uterus to the inner aspect of your abdomen (where your groin is). These ligaments can spasm and cause sharp, shooting pains. If this happens, take some deep breaths and move slowly and carefully until it subsides, usually within a few minutes."
—K.N.

THE WHOLE TRUTH AND NOTHING BUT
Back pain starts early, too

You would think that back pain wouldn't start until your third trimester, when you've gained the most weight. Unfortunately, back pain often strikes in the second trimester. Even though you're not all that big yet, your pelvis is on an expansion mission. The ligaments supporting your abdomen become more pliable, and the joints between your pelvic bones soften. The result: your aching back.

ADVICE FROM THE TRENCHES
Try yoga

"I never tried yoga before but had heard so much about it being good for pregnant women, so I got a prenatal tape (so I could make a fool out of myself in private!), and it was wonderful. Twenty minutes a day took care of my backache. I later signed up for a prenatal class. This is also a great way to meet expecting moms in your area."
—Beth, mom to Scott

day 145

DOCTOR'S ORDERS
Dealing with backaches

"Gentle stretching, warm but not hot baths, and massage by your partner can help relieve the day's aches and pains. Some women get sciatica, which is named after the nerve that travels from each buttock down each leg. You may experience sharp radiating pain—from mild to severe—shooting down one leg. Sitting can make it worse. Ice can help, or try using a tennis ball to massage the buttocks area. If your partner isn't around, you can lie on your back on the floor, placing the ball under the side bothering you. Slowly roll the ball in deep motions and see where you get relief. Most of the time sciatica gets better as you get to your third trimester, but if it doesn't, or if it's really severe, ask for a referral to a physical therapist."
—K.N.

TO-DO LIST
Moisturize like crazy

As you stretch out, the itchy skin begins. This is why women in their third trimesters rub their bellies all the time. By that point, they either don't realize they're doing it or they're so over it, they don't care if anyone's watching. You need a thick creamy lotion to coat your belly a few times a day.

ADVICE FROM THE TRENCHES
Try some scented oil

"My husband used to rub oil on my belly at night. It made us feel intimate when I felt too uncomfortable to have sex. It helped with the itching, too."
—Nadine, mom to Kalia

day 144

TO-DO LIST
Establish a no-sharing food policy

One of the benefits of being in your second trimester is that you are no longer required to share food with anyone, no matter how guilty they try to make you feel. You are exempt even from giving bites and tastes. From now on when you order dessert, specify, "One fork and a stun gun, please."

ADVICE FROM THE TRENCHES
The joy of eating

"My girlfriend and I were out to lunch. She was just hitting her third trimester, and I had just started my second and could finally eat again. When the waiter came for the second time to see if we were finished, I pointed to the garnish and pickle on my plate and said, 'When that's gone, you can bring over the dessert tray.'"
—Laurie, mom to Anthony Jr.

DOCTOR'S ORDERS
Don't avoid healthy fats

"In our culture, we're conditioned to avoid fats. As I mentioned earlier, healthy fats are important to your baby's normal brain development. Try to add such foods as almonds, walnuts, avocados, and salmon in moderation to your diet. Not only is the fat in these foods good for you, it will help keep you feeling full longer."
—K.N.

AT THIS POINT
You may be craving chocolate

The December 1992 issue of *Appetite* reported what you probably already know— women are more likely to crave sweets during the second trimester than at any other point in pregnancy.

day 143

TO-DO LIST
Get some good quality chocolate!

Go ahead and satisfy that chocolate craving. Bestselling author Dr. Andrew Weil recommends you skip the M&Ms and look instead for a good quality dark chocolate with at least 70 percent cocoa. You can find this chocolate in health food stores or specialty chocolate shops—it still has sugar in it, but the chocolate is better for you, and it includes the same kind of antioxidants found in red wine and green tea. Also, it contains fat that doesn't raise cholesterol levels.

AT THIS POINT
Your baby may benefit from chocolate, too!

Researchers in Finland asked three hundred pregnant women to record their stress levels and chocolate consumption, and then followed the children after birth. Results of the study were published in an April 2004 issue of *New Scientist* and showed that at six months of age, the babies of women who ate chocolate during pregnancy smiled and laughed more often. The researchers speculated that the positive effects could stem from the chemicals in chocolate. Hmm . . . if you want to test this theory, just watch out for the extra caffeine!

DOCTOR'S ORDERS
Stick with the real thing

"You may be tempted to eat low-fat or low-carb foods in an effort to stave off extra pounds. The truth is you need your carbohydrates, and most sugar substitutes have unhealthy chemicals. We don't know the full effects of these substitutes. Except for adding empty calories, plain old sugar is fine in your tea!"
—K.N.

day 142

AT THIS POINT
What should you be eating?

Okay, so you can't eat chocolate (or French fries, pizza, and donuts) every day. But what *should* you eat? According to the American College of Obstetricians and Gynecologists, a pregnant woman needs:

* Three or more servings of protein (lean meat, eggs, beans).

* Nine or more servings of whole grains like bread and cereal.

* Seven or more servings of fruits and vegetables.

* Three or more servings of milk and milk products, such as yogurt.

While this might seem like an awful lot of chewing (especially the nine or more servings of whole grains), consider that the serving sizes are probably smaller than you expect. Six crackers or one slice of whole grain bread both constitute a single serving.

DOCTOR'S ORDERS
Boost your protein intake

"You need about 70 to 75 grams of protein a day, which is easier than you think. If you eat three servings of lean protein and at least four servings of milk or milk products, you're two-thirds of the way there. The rest can be made up with snacks of protein-rich almonds, walnuts, or pumpkin seeds. Sneak some extra eggs in your diet: For example, instead of toast, make French toast. Add an extra egg to pancake batter. Add a chopped hard-boiled egg to your salad. Throw in some beans while you're at it."
—K.N.

day 141

TO-DO LIST
Make a smoothie

Tired of chewing all day long? Smoothies to the rescue! Smoothies taste great and are a fabulous way to sneak extra fiber, calcium, and protein into your diet without noticing. In a blender combine:

> $1/2$ cup (118 ml) frozen or fresh blueberries
>
> $1/2$ cup (118 ml) low-fat vanilla yogurt
>
> $1/2$ cup (118 ml) low-fat milk
>
> Optional: 1 tablespoon (14 ml) milled flax seed, for extra fiber and protein

THE WHOLE TRUTH AND NOTHING BUT
Is it okay to supplement?

Your main source of protein should always come from food, but ask your doctor if it's okay to boost your protein intake by adding a good quality supplement to a morning smoothie. Steer clear of protein bars—they often have tons of sugar. Look for a good powdered protein supplement that's just protein, with no or very little added sugar—or anything else.

AT THIS POINT
Is fish safe?

In your quest to eat more protein, you may be wondering about the safety of fish. As of March 2004, the USFDA recommends that pregnant women avoid shark, swordfish, tilefish, and king mackerel because of high mercury levels (which are bad for baby). Five fish that are low in mercury are shrimp, canned "light" tuna, salmon, pollock, and catfish. Be aware that canned "albacore," or "white," tuna has more mercury than canned "light" tuna, and it's advised that you eat no more than one serving a week while pregnant.

20 Weeks Pregnant!

HOW TO CELEBRATE THE HALFWAY MARK

Your countdown is half over! Only 20 weeks to go. You know how your S.O. got to do victory laps around the dining room table? You get to do laps, too—only in your favorite store, while shopping for a really cool (read: expensive) maternity outfit. You deserve it.

AT THIS POINT
The baby is ready for head-to-toe measurements

Now that your baby is bigger—a whole 9 ounces (255 grams) or more—and uncurling his legs, he can be measured from head to toe. Right now, your baby is 10 inches (25 cm) long from head to toe. Nerve cells for his senses are developing in specialized areas of his brain.

DOCTOR'S ORDERS
Measuring your progress

"Around now, the rate that your uterus grows will become more regular, and your doctor or midwife will use this as a gauge for how your pregnancy is progressing. She will measure the size of your uterus from the pubic symphysis (pubic bone) to the top of your uterus (fundus). This distance is measured in centimeters and should be equal to the number of weeks you are, give or take two centimeters. This is not an exact science, but it helps you follow the growth of your baby. If the measurements are off for two visits, don't panic; your doctor will order an ultrasound and see if a discrepancy truly exists."
—K.N.

TO-DO LIST

Make the critical underwear decision

Over or under? Now that you're getting big in the belly, wide in the behind, and "hippier," it's becoming quite clear that your days in normal, or the next size up, underwear are numbered. One of the toughest decisions in pregnancy—whether to wear maternity underwear above or below what used to be your waistline—must be made.

Over-the-Belly Advantages: Comfort. Comfort. Comfort. As you get bigger, over-the-belly maternity underwear—which hilariously are still called "briefs"—are frightening looking. Then again, who's going to see you? Your S.O. is already afraid of you, and your doctor or midwife has seen it all, so you might want to dive into the comfort of full-coverage undies with a nice wide crotch and be done with it.

Under-the-Belly Advantages: Comfort, sexiness, and the ability to expose your bump without exposing your underwear, too. If you found low-waisted underwear comfortable before pregnancy, and many do, you will probably stick with "under" underwear. You may still even fit into your pre-pregnancy pairs. Eventually though, as your belly expands, and your hips and butt expand with it, you will need maternity underbelly underwear, which has a spandex band to support your tummy from below.

If you already have a child, giving up sexy undies is not a problem, since you probably gave them up years ago. But if this is your first baby, you may not be ready to give up your nice bikini underwear and low-rise jeans. And if you feel great in them, why should you give them up? Whatever makes you feel best is the winning choice.

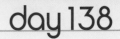

AT THIS POINT
You can't surrender your thongs (yet)

There are two kinds of women in the world: those who spend their lives trying to keep their underwear *out* of their behinds and those who swear it's more comfortable *in* their behinds.

If you're in the latter camp, you'll be thrilled to learn that you can buy maternity thongs. Though *maternity* and *thong* may be two words that you would never expect to find in the same sentence, some pregnant women swear by them and claim they're very comfortable and lend to the goddess feeling (even if the thongs themselves look like sling shots that could propel a small animal).

You can even buy thongs that go over the belly now, too—though you just may not look as sexy in them these days.

DOCTOR'S ORDERS
Watch out for UTIs

"Some studies show that thongs may increase the risk of bacterial vaginosis and urinary tract infections. Both of these types of infections can have implications in pregnancy. Having said that, if you haven't experienced these problems, you don't have to stop wearing them if you choose. Some of my patients find them more comfortable and swear by them. Feeling good underneath counts too!"
—K.N.

ADVICE FROM THE TRENCHES
You know your life is changing

"My husband really knew our lives were changing when I came home from my first shopping spree from Motherhood and my underwear was bigger than his."
—Marianne, mom to Patrick and Andrew

 # day 137

THE WHOLE TRUTH AND NOTHING BUT
Trendy equals expensive

As you go maternity clothes shopping, you'll quickly discover that *trendy* in maternity wear is code for *expensive*. Specialty stores have great maternity clothes, but they're pricey. The good news is (and this really burns up moms who were pregnant years ago) many department stores and discount megastores now sell very affordable and hip-looking maternity clothes. So shop around. This is no time for shopping snobbery.

TO-DO LIST
Go slumming before swimming

You thought buying a bathing suit when not pregnant was bad.

If you're going to be pregnant in the summertime, you're going to need a decent bathing suit, and finding one you like is a nightmare because the only one you'll like will be the pink keyhole tankini that costs an arm and a leg. Bummer.

Though in your normal life, you would *never* buy a used bathing suit, you're *not* normal, and you're going broke on maternity clothes. Swallow your pride and hit the consignment stores and even a garage sale or two. Look at it this way: After childbirth you'll have no pride, so why not reap the benefits now?

ADVICE FROM THE TRENCHES
Bathing beauty? Not!

"When it comes to bathing suits, the colored and polka dot ones make you look like an Easter egg with hair and legs. Until someone invents the all-in-one maternity raincoat bathing suit, stick with black."
—Kate, mom to Julia and Ellie

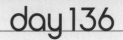

THE WHOLE TRUTH AND NOTHING BUT
Should you expose your bump or not?

If you read the celebrity magazines, you'll see a lot of bare bumps. But you should know this is a trend launched by pregnant celebrities after Jennifer Aniston played a pregnant woman on the TV show *Friends*. Thus, the bare umbilicus trend was started by a celebrity exposing a *fake* bump, and now largely remains a trend among celebrities who have personal trainers, shoppers, chefs, and lots of dough. Think about it! Have you ever seen a real pregnant woman baring her bump, even on the beach? Do you want to be the first?

Then again, this is your one chance to let your belly hang out and have it be considered attractive, sexy, and most importantly, *not fat*. So if you want to, go for it.

AT THIS POINT
Your fundus feels humongous

Speaking of bumps. By now, the top of your uterus is at the level of your bellybutton. You've likely gained between 10 to 15 pounds (4.5–6.8 kg). You will continue to gain an average of 1 pound (450 g) each week.

TO-DO LIST
Buy a sexy, form-fitting maternity top

You have to have one or two (okay, ten) really colorful, fun, trendy, low-cut and form-fitting maternity tops to enjoy in your second trimester, especially if you never had breasts before and have them now.

AT THIS POINT

You may need to dress up

Dressing up for a night out can be a nightmare of indecision even when you're not pregnant. And when you are pregnant, here's what you can do. Buy—or borrow—a simple black maternity dress that lands just above your knees. If you have the arms for it, make it sleeveless. That way, your naked arms and your legs (dressed in sheer black stockings) will break up the "bowling ball" look that affects so many pregnant women. Just accent with a bold necklace or silk scarf, and you're good to go. You can wear this dress to work (with a jacket or blouse) to stretch your wardrobe dollars.

HOW TO MAKE A SNOOKIE BROOKIE

Now that you have your fabulous new maternity outfit, it's time to party. But what can you drink, since alcohol is now off-limits? Forget ginger ale and non-alcoholic beer. Try a "mocktail" like a Snookie Brookie (blend 1 scoop vanilla ice cream, 3 ounces orange juice, and 3 ounces club soda until smooth).

ADVICE FROM THE TRENCHES
The last good night's sleep I had

"You have to pee, you cramp up, you wake up and need a snack, the baby moves . . . sleep deprivation begins early in pregnancy. It must be nature's way of preparing you for interrupted sleep when the baby arrives. I found napping as important in my second and third trimesters as in my first, so don't let the chance to snooze pass you by."
—Diane, mom to Robin and Ebon

THE WHOLE TRUTH AND NOTHING BUT
There's no "good side" for sleeping

You may hear that you should only sleep on your left side. It's true that lying on your left side will optimize your circulation and blood flow. But you shouldn't sleep only on your left side because you're trying to do the best for your baby. Relax and lie on whatever side is comfortable.

DOCTOR'S ORDERS
Tune in to your baby's sleep/wake cycle

"By now, you may be aware that your baby's movements have a pattern to them. Even at this early age, babies have their own sleep/wake cycles. Typically you may notice that there hasn't been movement for thirty minutes or an hour and then all of a sudden, the baby is wildly kicking. Unfortunately, your baby may like to sleep when you're awake and then as soon as you go to bed, start his gymnastic routine."
—K.N.

day 133

TO-DO LIST
Look at a large banana

Yep, you guessed it! This is the length of your baby
right now—almost 7 inches (18 cm) crown to rump, or
about the length of a banana. Right now, she weighs
around 10.5 ounces (297 grams). In the next few
weeks, she'll be putting on even more of her much-
needed baby fat. Her tongue, which, of course, she
will never, ever stick out at you, is now fully formed.

HOW TO STAND UP WITHOUT FEELING DIZZY

You may feel dizzy or lightheaded now when you stand up or put your head
down—that's because your cardiovascular system is changing to accommodate
your little one. Your blood pressure reaches its lowest levels in the second trimester.
If you get lightheaded, stand still for a moment and let it pass. If it doesn't pass,
sit down and put your head between your knees.

AT THIS POINT
You've probably felt a Braxton Hicks contraction

Braxton Hicks contractions usually start around now. They get their name from the
English doctor who first described them in 1872. Before that, they were called "that
sudden tightening over your belly that made you drop your hoe or stop churning
the butter." Braxton Hicks are harmless but can be uncomfortable. Each one can
last a few minutes to several minutes.

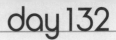

HOW TO STOP A BRAXTON HICKS CONTRACTION

Here is one of the key differences between a Braxton Hicks contraction and a real contraction—you can't stop the real ones. Braxton Hicks, on the other hand, stop on their own or can often be banished by changing your activity, breathing deeply, or drinking lots of water.

DOCTOR'S ORDERS
Know when to call for help

"Braxton Hicks may be uncomfortable, but they don't dilate your cervix. They aren't painful, but the tightening can feel intense. If this is your first pregnancy and you don't know the difference, make sure you don't ignore contractions that intensify and increase in frequency. This can be a sign of premature labor, and you should call your doctor."
—K.N.

THE WHOLE TRUTH AND NOTHING BUT
Ain't nothing like the real thing

You will read that Braxton Hicks contractions can be as painful as the real thing. Some people call them "practice" contractions. But as you will discover, that's sort of like saying Little League baseball is "practice" for the World Series.

day 131

TO-DO LIST
Sign up for childbirth classes now

Speaking of contractions, you should start looking for a childbirth class and sign up now for your third trimester—in case there's a waiting list or a class size limit. Your doctor or midwife can usually recommend a good one, and many hospitals have classes now as well. Classes are done in two or three sessions or one daylong session. You know how you're wondering how you'll know when you're really in labor? Childbirth education classes give you that information, breathing and relaxation techniques, information about pain medication, and much more.

HOW TO FIND OUT ABOUT NATURAL CHILDBIRTH CLASSES

Natural childbirth is birth that is unassisted by pain medication and with minimum medical intervention. Your midwife or doctor can usually recommend a class. There are various approaches. One of the most popular is Lamaze, which focuses on relaxation techniques and intensive practice in conditioning your response to pain. (This is where the whoosh-whoosh, or panting, breathing you see on TV originates.) Surprisingly, the Lamaze approach does not take a hard line for or against drugs, but rather emphasizes an informed decision (www.lamaze-childbirth.com).

DOCTOR'S ORDERS
You will need some help

"Whatever your desire for pain management, or no matter what childbirth approach you are comfortable with, you will need some tools—either medication or relaxation techniques—to help you deal with the early and most difficult part of labor. Start educating and preparing yourself early."
—K.N.

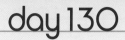
ADVICE FROM THE TRENCHES
Don't miss the hospital tour

"Knowing where to enter and where to go, seeing the labor rooms and all the equipment ahead of time, really made me feel more prepared and less nervous when it was time to go to the hospital for real."
—Dara, mom to Evan

AT THIS POINT
You may be tempted to skip the class

With so many books, magazines, and Web sites devoted to pregnancy, you may be tempted to skip the childbirth education class. The truth is, even a video can't replace a class. Most importantly, it gives you the opportunity to ask questions and visit the hospital if that's where the class is being held. Many times, childbirth educators are labor nurses or midwives, and they have so much inside information to share, you don't want to miss out. Here's another plus—it gives you a chance to meet other pregnant couples in your area.

TO-DO LIST
Consider a breastfeeding class, too

While you're signing up for a childbirth education class, consider a breastfeeding or lactation class as well. Even if you aren't sure you want to breastfeed, the more you learn about it, the better prepared you are to make an educated decision about whether or not it's right for you. This way, you'll feel more comfortable in your decision either way.

day 129

AT THIS POINT
Your baby is getting ready to poop

Your baby is already making meconium—a.k.a. the frightening black poop that will appear in his first few diapers. This sticky stuff is a combination of digestive secretion and amniotic fluid that he's swallowed. Some babies do pass it in utero during delivery, which of course those sparkling clean newborns on TV never do.

Believe it or not, in 129 days, poop is going to become one of your favorite subjects. (Oh yes it will.)

THE WHOLE TRUTH AND NOTHING BUT
A real pain in the butt

Constipation is a pain in the butt during pregnancy—pun totally intended. Thanks to progesterone (which slows digestion) and your growing uterus (which compresses your intestine), regular bowel movements will become a challenge.

In order to move things along, you need to be drinking as much as you can without floating away—at least ten glasses of water every day. Daily walking—or any exercise—helps a lot. (Doctors aren't sure why, they only know that people who don't exercise get constipated.)

But the most important thing you can do to alleviate constipation is to eat a fiber-rich diet. Fiber is not digested by your body—it passes through and helps to alleviate constipation. You need both soluble fiber (oat bran, beans, peas, and psyllium husk) and insoluble fibers (whole wheat products). Soluble fiber absorbs liquid and forms a gel, while insoluble fiber does not. Many fruits and vegetables contain both.

HOW TO SNEAK MORE FIBER INTO YOUR DIET

You need about thirty grams of fiber a day when you're pregnant. Considering that even most non-pregnant people don't get close to that amount, getting all of your fiber can be a challenge, even with a good supplement (see below). Here are some tips:

* Eat a handful of nuts and fruit for a snack.

* Don't drink fruit juice—eat the fruit instead (the one exception is prune juice).

* Put raw spinach or kale on your sandwich instead of lettuce.

* Eat baked beans as a side dish.

Some fiber-rich foods have the added benefit of protein:

* Put a tablespoon of ground flax into a smoothie, or mix into yogurt.

* Add beans, seeds, or nuts to salad.

* Eat split pea or lentil soup for lunch.

TO-DO LIST
Get a psyllium supplement

Psyllium is a safe fiber supplement. It's not a laxative—which you should avoid during pregnancy. The brands you can buy in the grocery store—like Citracel and Metamucil—work, but they have additives, dyes, and sugar. You can buy supplements without the additives in health food or vitamin stores.

If you supplement with psyllium, start slowly, once a day for a few days. If you don't notice improvement, work your way up to twice a day.

The trick with psyllium is that you have to mix it with water and drink it quickly because it gels and gets thick and unpleasant.

day 127

DOCTOR'S ORDERS
Relieve constipation safely

"Constipation can make you miserable. Always start with good old-fashioned prunes (now labeled "dried plums") or prune juice. You can then try a stool softener, like docusate sodium, but even this can take some time. Sometimes you need the big guns to get things going. If you need immediate relief, drink milk of magnesia or use a dulcolax suppository. Enemas are all right to use but may be difficult to administer. Not all S.O.s are up for the task. Once you get things going, try to maintain adequate fiber to keep this from happening again."
—K.N.

ADVICE FROM THE TRENCHES
Make your snacks count

"I made a great rule for myself during pregnancy that I continue to follow today: Don't eat anything, including snack foods like tortilla chips or crackers, unless it contains fiber. Switch to blue corn chips—they taste great. Dip them into refried beans and salsa and you've got a great, healthy snack."
—Clare, mom to Annie and Grace

HOW TO GET YOUR S.O. TO EAT BETTER, TOO

Make a pact with your S.O. to eat more healthfully. If he resists, don't announce it, just do it. If you're using whole grain pasta or brown rice, why bring it up? Just serve it and enjoy. He may not even notice.

HOW TO VISUALIZE YOUR BABY

Forget the fruit bowl. At 7$1/2$ inches long (19 cm), crown to rump, and a little over 12 ounces (340 grams) in weight, your baby really looks like a baby now. His primary teeth, which hopefully won't require braces later, have already formed beneath his gums. Here's an interesting detail—though his eyes are developed, his iris still has no color. By now, his sense of touch is well established. He may cultivate this sense by stroking his own face. His liver is functioning, and his pancreas has begun producing insulin.

THE WHOLE TRUTH AND NOTHING BUT
You're the one who is ripe

Now, you're the fruit. Make that a pear—but with breasts. Though you feel ripe all over, you may still be relatively small on top, but your bottom part is getting rounder and wider. (Still better than a cantaloupe.) Yes, you're probably getting uncomfortable—but look at the bright side. You can likely still bend over, tie your own shoes, and get out of your chair without two people pulling you. Things are looking good.

AT THIS POINT
Your innie may now be an outtie

As your uterus continues its expansion upward and outward, your bellybutton may pop out—way out—and stay that way until delivery. The breathing issue mentioned on day 169 may now be a lot worse; as your lungs get more cramped, you'll have to work harder to breathe.

But even if you can't breathe, so what? You're more than halfway through your pregnancy.

THE WHOLE TRUTH AND NOTHING BUT
The fruit may now be in your backside

Well, you could deal with just about anything Mother Nature was throwing your way, except maybe for that cherry- or lemon-sized hemorrhoid that suddenly has appeared in or around your backside.

Hemorrhoids—they can also be innies or outties—are common in pregnancy. Hemorrhoids are actually varicose veins (see below) of the rectum.

DOCTOR'S ORDERS
Dealing with hemorrhoids from hell

"Not what you needed! Hemorrhoids can be particularly bad in pregnancy because of all the pressure, constipation, and dilated veins. First address the issue of constipation, which causes or makes hemorrhoids worse. For comfort, try sitting in a bathtub and soak. Over-the-counter preparations are fine to use for added comfort. If the pain is severe, ask your doctor for prescription-strength medication. Most of the time these hemorrhoids will decrease in size and maybe even go away."
—K.N.

TO-DO LIST
Treat yourself to a massage

With your added aches, pain, and stresses (not to mention the hemorrhoids), you've got to treat yourself to a maternity massage. It's good for the body and mind. During a pregnancy massage, you lie either on your side or better yet, on a specifically designed pillow with a big belly cutout that makes it possible for you to lie on your stomach, no matter how huge you are.

You must make sure that your therapist is qualified in pregnancy massage. Talk with him or her beforehand.

AT THIS POINT
Back sleeping is for non-pregnant women

Now that you're in the second half of your pregnancy, your days of sleeping on your back are over (if they haven't ended already). Don't worry, you'll know when the time is right. How? Well, a distinct feeling of suffocation, from the weight of your uterus, will be a good tip-off. As will the dizziness and backache.

TO-DO LIST
Meet your new boyfriend

He doesn't have arms or legs and he can't bring you snacks, carry things for you, or make you laugh. But you will love him, and you will love him profoundly—let's call him Bob.

Bob is your new body pillow. If you don't have one already, *get one*. You will get into positions with Bob that will make your S.O. jealous.

A full body pillow is one of the truly great inventions for pregnancy. As your pregnancy progresses, it will be Bob and Bob alone that will help you sleep. Wrap your arms and legs around him, prop him under your belly or back, feel the support, and get some much-needed rest.

Many maternity stores sell these pillows, or you can browse different options online.

 # day 123

AT THIS POINT
Your dreams may be vivid and unpleasant

Here are three popular and very unpleasant second trimester pregnancy dreams:

1. You hear crying, and you can't find your baby.

2. Your insurance runs out while you're in labor.

3. Someone is yelling at you that you're doing something wrong.

HOW TO UNDERSTAND YOUR PREGNANCY DREAMS

It doesn't take Dr. Freud to figure out that pregnancy dreams are another way (besides flipping out on your S.O. for eating the last doughnut) to express all of your anxiety, stress, and excitement. According to psychologist and dream expert Patricia Garfield, author of *Women's Bodies, Women's Dreams*, it's common to dream of animals—particularly puppies, kittens, and cubs—during the second trimester. These dreams usually represent—well, let's take a wild guess—your thoughts toward your baby and your pregnancy!

But don't get freaked out if one of the kittens in your dream bites you or you ignore it. By now, hopefully you understand what a deeply conflicting experience pregnancy can be. Don't worry; a snappy kitten or snarling puppy may just represent your fears and anxiety coming out during sleep. If you have upsetting dreams like this, you're normal for a pregnant person, which of course means you're nuts by any other standard.

day 122

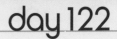

AT THIS POINT
You're worried about *striae gravidarum*

Though it sounds like a parasite you might get from eating raw food, *striae gravidarum* is in fact the stretch marks that all pregnant women dread. About 50 percent of all pregnant women get them, hate them, and try just about anything to make them go away.

Forget the cocoa butter, oils, and all the false promises. The only thing that can absolutely prevent stretch marks? Genetics. So if you want to avoid surprises, ask for a heads-up from your mother or grandmother.

TO-DO LIST
Order belly balm, anyway

Products with cocoa butter, mango butter, and olive oil won't prevent stretch marks, but they smell great and they also provide relief for the tummy itchies. Buying special creams can also help you feel pampered. But if you don't feel like shelling out for trendy belly creams, good old lotion found in your grocer's aisle will help the itchies just as well. Use a lot of it.

THE WHOLE TRUTH AND NOTHING BUT
Equal opportunity stretching

You may have already discovered that stretch marks can also occur on your breasts. And some women, when they look in the mirror, are surprised to discover stretch marks on their buttocks as well. Anywhere you're adding weight leaves you susceptible to stretch marks.

day 121

DOCTOR'S ORDERS
Don't sacrifice healthy eating for stretch marks

"Some women believe that if they don't gain a lot of weight, they won't get stretch marks. Again this is another aspect of pregnancy that is out of our control. The good news is that most stretch marks fade after pregnancy. With time they aren't as obvious as they are now. It's important to eat as healthfully as you can now and not worry about how big and stretchy you are."
—K.N.

AT THIS POINT
Is there hope for your belly postpartum?

Yes. Even if your stretch marks don't do you the courtesy of fading on their own, there are some things you can do—*after* you have your baby.

Retin-A has been shown to diminish stretch marks postpartum. Since its effects on breast milk are unknown, you should not use this during your pregnancy or while breastfeeding.

You may read about an herb called *centella asiatica* (Gotu Kola) that has been shown in limited studies to prevent stretch marks; however, its safety in pregnancy is unknown, and just as you should avoid all herbal remedies now, avoid this one, too.

Laser surgery may be an option, but you're certainly not going to want to do anything like that until you're finished having children.

ADVICE FROM THE TRENCHES
You won't have time to fret

"I look at it this way: I wasn't in a bikini before I had my boys, and I'm not in one now. It's really not such a big deal to have some marks on your belly. Your priorities do change. You'll be so busy with your newborn, you won't even think about your tummy."
—Renee, mom to Steven and Anderson

THE WHOLE TRUTH AND NOTHING BUT
Two kids may be more like it

Okay, with the trouble sleeping, the hemorrhoids, and the ligament pain, it may be time for a family revision plan again. Four is a little too much: Two sounds good, very good!

AT THIS POINT
Why can't men get pregnant?

Why hasn't someone figured out how to impregnate a man?

Crazy as it may sound, some scientists have argued that male pregnancy is theoretically possible. Before you start shopping for male maternity underwear, remember that it's only possible *in theory*. As of now, the only known male animal species to give birth are sea horses, pipefishes, and sea dragons.

The fact is that a male pregnancy would be so dangerous that the risks would outweigh the benefits.

(You, however, are not so sure.)

day 119

TO-DO LIST
Start attributing some of your weight to the baby

Drum roll, please. . . . Your baby is now 1 pound (450 grams)! She's about 8 inches (20 cm) long from crown to rump and looks like a tiny doll, complete with fingernails and toenails. Now you know at least a pound of what you're carrying belongs to her.

THE WHOLE TRUTH AND NOTHING BUT
The roar of the vacuum cleaner

You'll hear that if you run a vacuum or go near a barking dog while pregnant, these sounds won't faze or startle your baby once she's born. But is it true?

It just might be. Psychologists at Johns Hopkins University have found that very premature babies born between weeks 24 or 25 respond to a variety of sounds, so they've concluded that their sense of hearing had to have already been well developed. Pregnant women have reported that the baby will kick in utero in response to a loud noise.

AT THIS POINT
You're the symphony

Forget the vacuum cleaner—right now *you're* the most interesting source of sound for your baby. Your blood is whooshing, your stomach is gurgling, your intestines are rumbling, and your voice is filtered through the amniotic fluid. You're noisy, not even counting your new gassiness. It's also been found that fetal heart rate slows when the mother is speaking—which suggests that the fetus hears, recognizes, and is calmed by your voice. See? You're already good at this mothering thing, and the baby isn't even born yet.

THE WHOLE TRUTH AND NOTHING BUT
Yet another work challenge

Just when you thought you couldn't get any more distracted at work! Thanks to swelling and fluid retention, your hands may feel numb and tingly, or your wrists may be achy. Now, even answering your e-mail can be a challenge, and for the one in four women who go on to develop pregnancy-related carpal tunnel syndrome, usually in the second half of pregnancy, it may be painful.

Though typing on a keyboard at work probably didn't cause your problem, it can aggravate it. Wear a supportive wrist band (available at any drugstore) and make sure your chair and keyboard are positioned so that you don't have to flex downward. Ask your boss to order you an ergonomic keyboard—this will keep your wrists in the optimal position to reduce strain.

HOW TO BECOME A WAHM

Many moms dream of finding opportunities to work at home. While it may not be realistic to think you can suddenly make your current salary by working part time from home, many work at home moms (WAHMs) earn enough income that staying at home is viable. Many moms have used their skills to switch to careers in bookkeeping, party planning, child care, selling cosmetics or items for the home, proofreading, writing, tutoring, travel agenting, graphic design, computer programming, typing, and more. But remember, when surfing the Web or your local newspaper, don't get sucked in by ads that promise you can make hundreds of dollars in one week by working only a few hours or ones that require you to pay a fee for information or supplies—these are likely scams. If it sounds too good to be true, it is!

day 117

HOW TO SIT MORE COMFORTABLY AT WORK

Try to get up often and walk around for a few minutes. This will keep your circulation flowing when you sit back down. Keep your feet elevated, even when standing: have a low stool or sturdy cardboard box and put one foot up at a time.

AT THIS POINT
You might need support hose

If you're on your feet a lot for work, consider support hose, a.k.a granny panty-hose. These special stockings help relieve the pressure on your legs, which can be a big source of discomfort in Pregnancy Land.

Support hose are also known as *compression hosiery* because they help pump your blood back up to the heart, thereby reducing pain and swelling in the legs. They can provide relief if you have varicose veins (see Day 105). The compression on your legs should be graduated: greatest at the ankle and less so up your leg. There are also different levels of compression, so check with your doctor to see how much you may need. These hose tend to be expensive—but if you're experiencing discomfort, they're worth it.

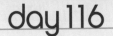

day 116

TO-DO LIST
Learn the difference between *kugel* and *kegel*

Kugel is a Jewish noodle pudding. It's really delicious, but unless you're eating it right now, it has nothing to do with your pregnancy.

A kegel is that funny little "squeeze squeeze" pelvic floor exercise developed by Dr. Arnold Kegel in the 1940s that helps you "bounce back" "down there." (Wink, wink.)

AT THIS POINT
Why do you need to do kegels?

Joking aside, kegels exercise your pelvic floor muscles and keep them strong. You need strong pelvic floor muscles to push your baby out. Once you have your baby, you need strong pelvic floor muscles so you won't have major urine leakage. Of course, there are sexual benefits, too.

DOCTOR'S ORDERS
Kegel like a pro

"To isolate your pubococcygeus muscle, which is one of the muscles you are contracting when you do a kegel, urinate in the toilet and stop the flow of urine. You are contracting your PC muscle. Don't do the exercises only on the toilet—just use it to locate the muscle. Try to do your kegels daily; the good news is that no one will know you're squeezing. Hold the contraction to the count of five (ten if you are really good) and release. Do this five times in a row. I tell my patients to pick a trigger phase or signal that reminds you to do your kegels, such as when someone asks you how you are or every time you hit a red light."
—K.N.

day 115

AT THIS POINT
Your S.O. may be begging you to kegel some more

Unlike the mucus plug, hemorrhoids, and colostrum, kegel exercises are one pregnancy subject that men love to talk about, hear about, and encourage—even nag—you to do. Why? Because your S.O. doesn't want to think he'll be putting his penis in something the size of the Lincoln Tunnel after you give birth. (He's got a point, don't you think?)

THE WHOLE TRUTH AND NOTHING BUT
Kegels can only do so much

Kegels do work, but let's face it—you're passing a person from the inside of your body to the world outside. There's going to be some stretching and leakage issues postpartum. Even if you do your kegels a hundred times a day, every day, from now on, you should know that many women still pee a little when they sneeze or laugh. It doesn't mean that you'll pee yourself in public, or that your sex life will go out the window; it's just that a baby is big, even when small.

HOW TO DO YOUR KEGELS WITHOUT COMPLAINING

Apparently, modern day kegels are nothing like what Dr. Kegel intended. He actually invented a biofeedback device called a *perineometer* that helped women to do these exercises more effectively. Let's reemphasize the word *device* here, 'cause guess where it used to go? See, simple squeezing isn't so bad after all!

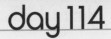
HOW TO PREPARE YOUR PUP FOR BABY

For many dog lovers, their pet is considered the first baby of the house. So in all fairness to your dog (who is about to get dethroned), you're going to need to provide help adjusting to a newborn. Experts agree that the sooner you get started working with your pet to help her adjust, the better. Ask your veterinarian for some training tips.

TO-DO LIST
Hire a trainer

If your pet is already unruly, you may want to consider professional help—the situation will only get worse when the baby arrives. Search online or talk with friends for recommendations for a trainer in your area.

DOCTOR'S ORDERS
Don't forget to pet your cat

"It is important for pregnant women not to change the cat's litter because of the risk of toxoplasmosis, a parasite that can cause birth defects. Otherwise cats are safe. Just remember to give them attention during and after pregnancy so they don't leave you any revenge 'gifts.'"
—K.N.

day 113

HOW TO DEAL WITH BELLY TOUCHING

Some women don't mind the extra attention from strangers in public, especially during the second trimester, when being bumpy is still fun. But it can get tiring, and by the third trimester, the belly touching has gotta go!

By the end of your third trimester—especially if your due date has come and gone—you will probably have a look on your face that will scare the belly touchers away. But if you're bugged by belly touchers now, what can you do? It's not like you can stop grocery shopping. When dealing with strangers, you have much more leeway to be rude or shocking:

You can say: "Um, do you realize that's actually my uterus you're feeling?" That realization often scares people away and makes them think twice. Or just cry "Ow!" whenever someone touches you; it will teach the grabbers to think twice.

The only surefire way to prevent touching before it starts is to tell people straight out, "Please, don't touch me."

TO-DO LIST
Buy a "No Touching Belly" T-shirt

If you really want to get the "no-touch" message across, consider buying a maternity T-shirt that says "Hands off Belly," "Hands off Junior," or other similar messages. Any T-shirt shop will be glad to create the shirt for you.

TO-DO LIST
Borrow a soccer ball

Don't kick that soccer ball—just hold it in your hands. To describe your uterus, we must turn to the world of sports. This week, your uterus is the size of a soccer ball and is now an inch (2.5 cm) above your bellybutton. Yep, that's big!

AT THIS POINT
Speaking of big . . .

Your baby weighs about 1 pound, 3 ounces (539 g) and measures around 8½ inches (21 cm) tall. He has a sense of equilibrium; he can tell the difference between upside down and right side up. His big job over the next few weeks is to add blood vessels to his lungs, which will prepare them for the job of getting oxygen into his blood.

THE WHOLE TRUTH AND NOTHING BUT
The glucose screening test

A glucose screening test screens for gestational diabetes, a high blood sugar condition that can affect your pregnancy if it goes undetected. It's not painful, but it's a pain because you have to drink a very sweet (read: icky) drink and then have your blood sugar level drawn one hour later. If this value comes back too high, you will need to do the three-hour glucose tolerance test, which tests your levels when you are fasting and then one, two, and three hours after you drink even more sugar. If two values are abnormal, you have gestational diabetes.

day 111

DOCTOR'S ORDERS
Managing gestational diabetes

"The good news is that gestational diabetes can be managed with a specific diabetic diet. While most sweets and simple carbohydrates won't be allowed, you will be happy to know your baby will be fine. Rarely, gestational diabetes isn't controlled with diet alone, and insulin may be prescribed. This can be scary and overwhelming, but again, with close management you can expect a healthy outcome, so hang in there."
—K.N.

THE WHOLE TRUTH AND NOTHING BUT
Even your nose can't escape

In Pregnancy Land, even your nose is not safe. If you're still keeping track, the hormone to blame this one on is estrogen. High levels of estrogen cause swelling in your mucous membranes. Your blood volume is increasing all over the place, even in your nose, which causes your blood vessels to expand, resulting in a stuffy nose.

HOW TO GET SINUS RELIEF

Some people swear by neti pots for dealing with clogged sinuses—they look like old-fashioned bottles that might have a genie inside, which you fill with warm water. These help you flush your sinuses. So what if you feel like you're trying to get the genie out of the bottle by sucking him up your nose and then blowing him out again?

day 110

ADVICE FROM THE TRENCHES
Dealing with nose misery

"You're going to buy a humidifier for your baby, so buy it sooner rather than later. It will help your sinuses and also your dry skin."
—Sima, mom to Rohit

DOCTOR'S ORDERS
Apply gentle pressure if your nose bleeds

"You may get occasional nosebleeds as a result of dilated blood vessels in the nose. Don't be alarmed if this happens. Simply apply gentle pressure with a towel or washcloth, and this too shall pass."
—K.N.

THE WHOLE TRUTH AND NOTHING BUT
Speaking of bleeding mucous membranes . . .

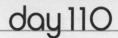

Another surprise is waiting for you in Pregnancy Land—bleeding and tender gums. For the same reason your nose may bleed, the increased pressure on your blood vessels may affect the way your gums react to the bacteria in plaque. This is called *pregnancy gingivitis*, and about half of all pregnant women experience it.

What you can do: Brush with a softer toothbrush, and floss more frequently. Try an antibacterial mouth rinse to keep plaque in check. Buy a toothbrush with a rubber tip. After you brush, run the rubber tip around your gum line to remove excess plaque.

Make sure to keep up with your dental care while pregnant. You may need an extra professional cleaning during pregnancy if your gums worsen. Let your dentist know you're pregnant.

day 109

HOW TO DO THE LINEA NIGRA!

No, it's not the new line dance that you tried at your cousin's wedding. It's what may be happening, or will happen, on your abdomen. In many pregnant women, a line of dark skin forms down the middle of their abdomen.

Yes, it fades after childbirth.

AT THIS POINT
Your areola may also be *nigra*

There may be more than just a dark line on your body—there may also be some dark circles now orbiting your breasts. These would be your former nipples. Pregnancy darkens them, too. They will return to previous pinkness once this science project is over.

THE WHOLE TRUTH AND NOTHING BUT
Wacky pregnancy symptom #4,987

While you're doing the *linea nigra* and the *areola negra*, you might spy a strange little skin-like thing suddenly hanging on your body. Gently pull on it. If it comes off, it's lint. If it stays, it's a skin tag. Pregnancy can make these little protrusions of skin grow, and it can also inspire moles to grow or change. If a mole changes size, color, or shape, you need to have it checked out, just to be on the safe side.

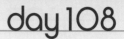

THE WHOLE TRUTH AND NOTHING BUT
One more wacky skin issue for this week

While we're talking about weird skin issues, you may also experience what's called "the mask of pregnancy." This is a nice way of saying you now have dark blotches on your neck and face, and you will feel like you need a mask *because now you look like a freak*. This condition is less common than *linea nigra,* but according to the American Academy of Dermatology, it occurs in up to 70 percent of pregnant women. Don't worry! The blotches really and truly go away after childbirth.

HOW TO MINIMIZE THE MASK

There is no known potion, cream, or magic spell to make the spots go away. One way to keep the weird facial spots off your face or keep them from darkening or proliferating is to lather yourself up in sunscreen, even in the winter months. If you're pregnant in the summer, you'll need a wide hat.

AT THIS POINT
You're getting it . . .

Pregnancy—especially your first pregnancy—is still mind-boggling and totally emotionally consuming. You live, breathe, and sleep pregnancy. It's a 24/7 job with no time off or mercy for good behavior.

day 107

AT THIS POINT
Don't admit your weight to anyone

As you will find, total strangers will have no qualms about asking you about your weight gain and then will make you feel bad no matter what you say. "What, you've gained 15 pounds already! My wife only gained 15 pounds for her whole pregnancy!" or "What, only 2 kilograms! Don't you think you better eat a little more so the baby isn't born too small?" Your best bet: Just refuse to be sucked in. Don't admit your weight gain. Say, "I'm really not sure." Of course, any mom will know this is a lie, but other pregnant moms will appreciate the tactic!

ADVICE FROM THE TRENCHES
Suddenly, everyone is a doctor

"Though I ignored a lot of what was said to me about my pregnancy, every once in a while, you do actually get a good piece of advice, so even though the constant opinions can be annoying, you never know when you might get a good tip."
—Margaret, mom to Shane and Colleen

TO-DO LIST
Start cashing in on your entitlements

If belly poachers, pokers, and bossy strangers are the *yin* in the universe, then people doing you favors because of your big belly are the *yang*. So let people carry your bags. Let your coworkers bring lunch back for you. Take any break you can get, and enjoy.

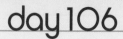

AT THIS POINT
Your S.O. may be acting overprotective

Your S.O. won't let you jaywalk, carry anything heavy, or leave the house without a homing device on. Though he may be treating you like an impaired person with no common sense, sense of direction, or cell phone, consider it from his point of view: You are pregnant, distracted, getting bigger and slower, and you keep losing your cell phone or forgetting to charge it. Maybe he's got a point.

TO-DO LIST
Get a new cell phone

Speaking of cell phones . . . If you have an older cell phone without the Global Positioning System (GPS) feature, you need a new phone. The GPS feature means no matter where you are (and in case you don't know where you are—which will be quite possible given your memory right now), emergency personnel can still find you. And while you're shopping for a new cell phone, a built-in camera feature will also come in handy when the baby arrives and he or she makes an amazingly cute face in the grocery store.

Just don't drive while talking on a cell phone—it's not safe for anyone, especially pregnant women, who are already distracted!

ADVICE FROM THE TRENCHES
Enjoy the attention while you have it

"With baby number one, my husband was so into the pregnancy—doctor's visits, making sure I was comfortable, and so on. But with number two he was like, 'Um, if you're going to whine like that, maybe you should go sleep in the guest room.'"
—Elizabeth, mom to Nathan and Justin

day 105

AT THIS POINT
What's happening with your baby?

Your baby may already have a distinct hair color (although it's common for this color to change once she's born or during her first year of life). She's just around 9 inches (23 cm) long from crown to rump, and she's nearly 1 pound, 5 ounces (595 grams). That lean machine still has much fat to add, which will help her fill out and lose the wrinkled raincoat look over the next several weeks. Her bones are hardening, and her brain is still growing at a rapid speed.

THE WHOLE TRUTH AND NOTHING BUT
Varicose veins

By now, you may have discovered varicose veins, especially on your legs. These veins need a name change to Varicose Villains, because they may be uncomfortable, even painful. They're rarely dangerous, however, but they're always really unsightly.

Varicose veins are caused by increased pressure on your leg veins from—what else?— increased blood volume and your soccer ball–sized uterus. Sometimes varicose veins do go away on their own within months of your baby's birth. Other times, they don't—and the only way to get rid of them is surgically.

Just like stretch marks, varicose veins are often genetic—so if you're destined to get them, there's not much you can do about them.

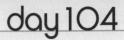

HOW TO TELL SPIDER VEINS FROM VARICOSE VEINS

If you have purplish or red veins on your legs or abdomen that are painless, thin, and spidery looking, these are spider veins, and they'll usually disappear after birth. Varicose veins bulge or appear as thick blue veins underneath the skin, usually on your legs. The biggest difference is that varicose veins can be quite painful during pregnancy.

DOCTOR'S ORDERS
Put your legs up

"There isn't a whole lot to do to prevent varicose veins other than avoid prolonged standing or lifting, which can aggravate the pressure on your veins. Try supportive stockings that aren't restrictive, and put your legs up whenever the opportunity arises. Exercise can help pump the pooled blood back to your heart, so try walking, even a short distance, every day."
—K.N.

THE WHOLE TRUTH AND NOTHING BUT
Volcanic vulva

Not only can you get varicose veins on your legs and your rectum (a.k.a. hemorrhoids—see day 125) but many women get them on their vulva, the external genitalia that includes the labia, clitoris, and vaginal opening. (OUCH.) Your vulva is a very sensitive place, so you will know pretty much right away if you have a bulging vein down yonder even if you can't see anything. Sometimes the pain can be very bad and can make sex painful. Sitting in the bath and then lying on your left side can soothe the discomfort and help the blood return to the heart, where it does only good things.

day 103

THE WHOLE TRUTH AND NOTHING BUT
Your butt may look pretty bad, too

If you are prone to cellulite, a nonmedical term for fatty deposits that cause dimpling on your skin, your butt and your thighs may end up looking like a bowl of cottage cheese. Yuck. Cellulite can strike even if you exercise and eat healthfully. Like stretch marks, varicose veins, and all of these lovely pregnancy side effects you weren't ready for, there isn't much you can do except wait it out. As you go back down weight-wise after your baby is born, the cellulite will probably go away on its own.

AT THIS POINT
"Oh, that's nothing!"

You could have a varicose vein on your vulva the size of a cucumber and there's always someone who's had one the size of an eggplant. No matter how much you're scratching, no matter how much of a Petri dish you feel like, there's always someone who can one-up you. You'll hear, "Oh, that's nothing! My daughter-in-law had to be dipped in balm, her skin got so dry . . ."

ADVICE FROM THE TRENCHES
The things people say

"There's nothing like being a twin when only one of you is pregnant. When I was 6 months pregnant, my twin, Lisa, and I were at her drycleaners. The girl behind the counter looks at us in a funny way. We think we know what's coming (yes, yes, we're twins . . . yes, yes, one of us is pregnant) when she asks if I'm Lisa's mother. I wanted to lunge over the counter and slap her."
—Meg, mom to Christopher, Patrick, and Erin

day 102

TO-DO LIST
Get on top

If you ever felt shy about trying some interesting positions during sex, here's the perfect reason—your big belly means the missionary position won't cut it anymore. Here are the most commonly used second-half pregnancy positions (with some more interesting names):

* **Reversal of Fortune**—You're now on top, and he's on the bottom. This gives you control over penetration, keeps the weight off of your tummy, and gives your S.O. a great view of your breasts.

* **Posterior Party Time**—This rear entry position has you on all fours with the man kneeling behind. But take it gently; this position allows for more penetration.

* **Spoon Swoon**—You're on your side with your back to your S.O.'s front. He enters from the rear, which keeps his weight off your tummy and keeps penetration on the shallow side, which might be more comfortable for you as you grow. In fact, you may find this so comfortable, you'll never go back!

DOCTOR'S ORDERS
You may have heard that . . .

". . . nipple stimulation can cause premature labor. While it's true that nipple stimulation in the form of sucking or rubbing can cause uterine contractions by releasing a hormone called oxytocin, these contractions are usually harmless as long as they don't get more intense and they stop. If they don't, call your doctor immediately, as this could be a sign of premature labor."
—K.N.

# day 101

THE WHOLE TRUTH AND NOTHING BUT

Leaky boob syndrome

It's possible to have some colostrum leakage now. Though most women don't experience any leakage until the third trimester (and some not at all until after the baby is born), it is possible to have some now, especially during sex. Colostrum is a thin, yellowish fluid containing antibodies that help protect your baby from infection. So you shouldn't worry about it, but it may come as a surprise, especially during sex! The best way to deal with it: Buy some nursing pads, available at drugstores, to put into your bra.

HOW TO DEAL WITH CRAMPUS INTERRUPTUS

During sex, be sure to move your legs around a lot, otherwise you might get a whopping leg cramp that will have you moaning for all the wrong reasons.

Whopping leg cramps can also cause *sleepus interruptus*. To prevent cramps, drink tons of water (what else?) and do some massage and hamstring stretches before bed or when they wake you up. The following stretches can help ease the pain in your calf and hamstring:

Calf muscle stretch: In a standing lunge with both feet pointed forward, straighten the rear leg. (Repeat with opposite leg.)

Hamstring muscle stretch: Sit with one leg folded in and the other straight out, foot upright and toes and ankle relaxed. Lean forward slightly and touch the foot of the straightened leg. (Repeat with opposite leg.)

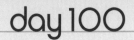

THE WHOLE TRUTH AND NOTHING BUT
Big beautiful breasts still MIA?

Some women find that after the 20-week midpoint, their breasts have another growth spurt. And then again, some do not—unless you count even more of those charming veins now visible all over your breasts as a spurt.

You may not notice a large increase in your size until after you give birth and your breast milk comes in. This lasts for about a week, and then your breasts usually go back down to the size you were in pregnancy. Many women (but of course not all) will not see additional breast growth from now until their breast milk comes in.

TO-DO LIST
Get fitted for a maternity bra

One bra manufacturer believes that as many as 70 percent of all women don't have the right-sized bra, so you can imagine how many women are walking around in Pregnancy Land with the wrong size. You really need to get measured now. At the very least, you should go to a store and try on as many bras as you can find. You don't want your bra to be too big, or it won't give you enough support.

ADVICE FROM THE TRENCHES
Fitting tip

"Buy a maternity bra that fits you now on the first clasp. That way you know you'll have room for expansion, especially after your milk comes in."
—Mary Judith, mom to Katelyn and Jordan

THE WHOLE TRUTH AND NOTHING BUT
You've been visited by the Nippleator

Did your nipples suddenly grow, so they now look like Frisbees? You've been visited by the pregnancy Nippleator, a.k.a. estrogen. You may also have flaking or bumps on your nipples. These bumps were there before; they're oil glands but now they're just bigger. Your nipples will go back to normal once pregnancy and breastfeeding are behind you.

HOW TO REALLY PREPARE FOR BREASTFEEDING

Physically, this is an easy one—there are no nipple push ups or toughening up to do. Mother Nature prepares your breasts and nipples for you. We've been telling men for years that size doesn't matter, and it doesn't matter for you, either. Big or small, most women are capable of breastfeeding.

The best way to really prepare for breastfeeding is in your head: Know that though it may be natural, breastfeeding often doesn't seem that way! In fact, getting started and sticking with it can be extremely hard. Ask a mom who breastfed, and she'll tell you that for the first week your nipples may crack, bleed, and even become infected. You may want to cry every time your baby is on your breast. Your baby may have trouble latching on for a few weeks.

This is why a lactation class at your hospital will help (if you still haven't signed up for one, do it now). This class will give you all the details about positioning, how infants suck, and how to tell by output (diapers) if your baby is getting enough input (breast milk).

AT THIS POINT
What's the baby up to?

He's about 1 1/2 pounds (680 grams) in weight and measures just around 9 1/2 inches (24 cm) long from crown to rump. At this point, his lungs are, or will soon be, developed enough for him to take small breaths of amniotic fluid. But he's just practice breathing; all of his oxygen comes through the placenta and umbilical cord until birth. His eyelids have been closed until now in order for the retinas to fully develop, but now his eyes are open—and he's even blinking.

Once born, you would never think to hold a baby upside down, but in utero it's comfortable. Usually, by the end of this trimester, thanks to gravity, your baby will start to settle in a head-down position. Some babies do not turn head down until late in the last trimester or what feels like the very last second.

HURRY UP AND WAIT ALERT
So close to the last trimester

You're probably getting very excited to be in your third trimester and to have two-thirds of your pregnancy behind you.

As you head into the last weeks of your second trimester, your uterus is now about 2 1/2 inches (6.4 cm) above your bellybutton. During the rest of your pregnancy, you will grow nearly 1/2 inch (1.3 cm) each week.

Most of your intestines, large and small, have been pushed up into your upper abdomen—which explains why your food seems to sit there during meals. Gas pains can really get you under the ribs. There isn't much to do but wait. Some yoga poses can help you make room for all those squished organs; just make sure you follow a safe prenatal program.

day 97

AT THIS POINT
Are you a klutz or what?

Yes, pregnancy makes you completely klutzy as well as forgetful, weepy, and emotional. You will drop more things in the next three months than you have in your whole life. As your baby grows, your center of gravity will be completely new, and this causes many pregnant women to have issues with tripping and falling. So hang on to those handrails on the way up *and* down the steps.

TO-DO LIST
Banish your Manolo Blahniks

If you're not Carrie Bradshaw from *Sex and the City*, you probably don't have a closet full of stiletto Manolos, but you do have some high heels, and by now, high may not be the wisest choice for someone who suddenly has more weight up high and out front.

THE WHOLE TRUTH AND NOTHING BUT
Relaxin may be stressing you out

Here's one pregnancy hormone that could use a name change—relaxin.

Relaxin is thus named because it relaxes the pelvic girdle and softens your cervix. Though it peaks much later in your pregnancy, its general presence has affected the ligaments and muscles in your body, including the ligaments in your feet that cause your bones to grow.

Though we commonly think of foot problems occurring later in pregnancy, when swelling sets in, many women find their feet have grown in the second trimester.

HOW TO DEAL WITH EXPANDING FEET

Let's see: Your feet are bigger and your shoes feel tight. So what should you do?

Buy new shoes, of course! This is one shoe spree you really can't help but go on. Wearing tight shoes will make you miserable, make it hard to walk, give you ingrown toenails, and make bunions come to life. With all the discomforts of pregnancy, this is one you can control.

THE WHOLE TRUTH AND NOTHING BUT
Your feet will keep growing

Many women may go up an entire shoe size by the time they have their babies. And in your next trimester, the swelling of your feet can worsen. But once all of the swelling subsides, you may find that you can get back into your old shoes.

AT THIS POINT
You're glowing, all right!

Your feet are growing, and your other extremities, your hands, are probably glowing. Though you still may not have that joyous pregnancy glow you were hoping for, at least one part of you is radiating—but unfortunately, it's the palms of your hands. You'll never believe this, but your suddenly bright red and itchy palms, and possibly the soles of your feet, were caused by increased estrogen. (But you already knew it's from increased estrogen because *what isn't caused by it and/or progesterone?*) If you're wondering what hormones don't do to you during pregnancy, the answer is *not much.*

day 95

THE WHOLE TRUTH AND NOTHING BUT
You can't win, even if you're in great shape

If you were a pre-pregnancy karate champ and you still want to kick ass in the gym and—more importantly—can safely and comfortably kick ass while pregnant, go for it. However, as you start to become more visibly pregnant, get ready for the comments: "Are you sure you should be doing that in your condition?" or "Have you asked your doctor if that's safe?"

Here are some comebacks for you:

"What condition?"

"I am a doctor!"

Remember, pregnant women get a special dispensation to lie.

AT THIS POINT
Weight becomes a competitive sport

Your newest form of exercise—the Pregnancy Comparing Game—is well under way. And though it's not fair, you're being thrown on the field with women who aren't even pregnant anymore!

Get a room of moms together and inevitably you'll hear, "I gained such and such with my first and such and such with my second." Not only are we obsessed with our weight during pregnancy, we love talking about it years later. Though we may have felt like big huge blobs at the time, if we're in reasonably good shape we love to gloat about how fat we were. If we didn't gain a lot, we love talking about that, too—throwing in, of course, how we ate like total pigs but just couldn't seem to put the weight on.

AT THIS POINT
You're realizing what you've said in the past

Now you know how it feels to have your stomach the subject of constant comment by friends, coworkers, and strangers. You're probably realizing that you may have said something to a pregnant woman in the past that made her feel badly or self-conscious. You didn't mean it, but unless you're pregnant you don't get how hurtful and tiring all the comments about your size can be. So even though some days it's a challenge, try to give others the benefit of the doubt, too.

HOW TO RESPOND TO COMMENTS WHEN YOUR HORMONES ARE RAGING

Comment: Wow, you're huge!
Response: Yep. *I'm* pregnant; what's your excuse?

Comment: Are you having twins?
Response: No, are you?

Comment: Are you due soon?
Response: Look at your watch and then say: "Any second now."

TO-DO LIST
Write a letter to Dear Abby

Dear Abby,

Can you please tell your readers that the only comment a pregnant woman wants to hear about her size is, "You look wonderful!"

Thank you,

Frustrated Pregnant Woman

THE WHOLE TRUTH AND NOTHING BUT
Uh oh, no name yet?

Still stuck? Still arguing? Still unsure? If you're wondering how you and your S.O. stand in relation to other couples choosing names, an informal poll of 122 expectant parents sponsored by the Web site All Info About Pregnancy found that:

34 percent of couples agreed on a name before birth

29 percent had the names picked out before pregnancy

7 percent couldn't agree at all

6 percent said they were waiting to see what the baby looked like

ADVICE FROM THE TRENCHES
She didn't look like anybody

"We had three possible names, and we thought that once our daughter was born, it would be clear which one we should pick. Well, it wasn't. But one of the nurses said, 'She looks like a Mary or an Abigail, and we looked at each other, and Mary it was!"
—Hope, mom to Mary, Kevin, and Vincent

TO-DO LIST
Shake some branches on your family tree

Call your oldest living relative and learn every relative's name you can. You may have had a great-great-grandmother named Alice or a great-uncle named Samuel that you can name the baby after. Naming your baby after an ancestor can add meaning to the naming process and is a wonderful way to honor family members, even if you didn't know them.

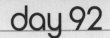
AT THIS POINT
I'm not going to be like that!

No doubt you're noticing mothers with their children a whole lot more than you did before. You probably already have some ideas of how you'll parent differently. For example, your child will never:

* have a tantrum in a grocery store (only brats do that)

* eat cookies in the grocery store (she will request carrot sticks)

* eat sugar or drink juice (she will request water or milk)

* get hooked on a binky (she will be a secure child)

You will also never in a million years tell your child, "If you don't get back in this grocery cart, I'm leaving. Okay, here I go. Okay, I mean it. See my keys are out. I'm shaking them. Here I go . . ."

THE WHOLE TRUTH AND NOTHING BUT
What real moms think of your plan

Good luck!

ADVICE FROM THE TRENCHES
Consider staying silent

"If I were you, I would keep my big child-rearing plans to myself—especially in front of mothers with young children. Maybe you will be the one mother in a million who continues to make her own organic baby food past the third batch and really won't use lollipops as a child-rearing tool. But then again, you haven't been shopping with a young child yet."
—Lisa, mom to Harris and Brian

day 91

HOW TO VISUALIZE YOUR BABY

By now, your baby is just about 2 pounds (900 g) and 10 inches (25 cm) long from crown to rump, and 14 to 15 inches (35–38 cm) tall from head to toe, which is about 1 inch (2.5 cm) taller than a Barbie or Ken doll. Your baby is almost fully developed, even down to her eyelashes. Her immune system is developing quickly. And that's good news, because as soon as you venture out with your baby in public, you'll be horrified by how many people cough and sneeze near her.

TO-DO LIST
Consider a last vacation or weekend getaway

This could be your last chance to travel somewhere and actually enjoy it. In another month, you won't want to be away from home, just in case. Besides, you'll be too big and tired to have fun. Think about it—once the baby comes, you're not going anywhere on vacation, alone with your S.O., for at least several months.

THE WHOLE TRUTH AND NOTHING BUT
They might not let you on the plane!

You may want to make your getaway by car. Some airlines do place restrictions on pregnant passengers. If you're flying and have a big belly, you need a doctor's or midwife's note to get on a plane. On some airlines, you may not be permitted to fly within thirty days of your due date or after week 32 without a doctor's note.

Call your airline and ask what the restrictions are. If you're carrying big, you may be stopped and questioned, so you may want to get a doctor's note just in case.

DOCTOR'S ORDERS
Air travel is safe but . . .

"You are usually safe to travel by plane until week 34, but even now, travel can be fairly uncomfortable given your size and the amount of swelling that can happen. Pregnant women are at risk for blood clots, especially when immobile, so it is important to remember to get up and walk the aisles for at least ten minutes every hour of the flight. From here on out, the real question is whether flying is absolutely necessary, and if it is, try to take every precaution—check with your doctor before leaving and know exactly where the closest hospital will be with the best medical technology."
—K.N.

THE WHOLE TRUTH AND NOTHING BUT
Fear may be settling in or intensifying

Fear of not being allowed to get on a plane may not be your only fear right now. As your second trimester ends and your third begins, reality sets in. You look at your stomach; you know about how big your vagina is; and you may be thinking, "Okay, a baby is going to come of there. That is going to hurt." That's pretty frightening. But it is not the same as thinking, "I can't do it" or "I'm not strong enough to handle it."

Labor is unknown, and the unknown—even when we very much want the end result—is scary. Being afraid doesn't mean you won't get through it, can't handle it, or can't have a positive experience. You're just being honest with yourself.

# day 89

ADVICE FROM THE TRENCHES

It's okay to be afraid

"Most of all, never let anyone tell you there's nothing to be afraid of, or that there's something wrong with you for being afraid. Pain is scary, and having any kind of medical procedure, including a birth, is always going to be unknown—even if you've been through it before. Would you go in for an appendectomy and not be at least a little afraid?"

—Dana, mom to Elsa and Maya

HOW TO DEAL WITH YOUR FEAR

Understand that the closer you get to your countdown day, you'll be more and more willing to go through labor. By then, enough is enough! Whether or not this is actual courage, it feels a lot like courage when the time comes, and that's what counts.

Don't keep your fears to yourself out of fear of judgment or of looking like a wimp. Make sure you're open and honest with your partner as well as your doctor or midwife. Becoming educated about the process and getting information from informed medical professionals will help you feel less fearful.

Seek out the company of a positive and supportive friend who has been through labor and who can offer you encouragement and support.

Above all, remember: Fear of labor is universal in Pregnancy Land.

DOCTOR'S ORDERS
Have faith

"Understanding that the fear of the unknown is far greater than the actual pain itself is important to hold on to. The good news about labor pain is that it doesn't usually start all at once with severe, sudden, intense pains. It usually starts with some erratic milder contractions. These are what I like to call practice contractions, which help you get used to the idea. As time progresses, if you are in labor, the contractions will become more regular and intense. You will get scared by the intensity, but if you have support around you, and you use your breathing techniques, you will handle them."
—K.N.

THE WHOLE TRUTH AND NOTHING BUT
Forget the pioneer

In your first 20 weeks of pregnancy, it's easy to think, "I can go natural; the pioneer women did it, so I can, too."

Then you start to get bigger and bigger and you may start to think, "Yes, but those pioneer women also had their teeth pulled with only a shot of whisky to ease the pain!"

If you're wavering, you're that annoying "N" word again—*normal*. Uncertainty is totally to be expected. Why not leave your options for pain medication open? It doesn't mean you're a wimp or not in touch with the power of your body. It just means that you're honestly facing an unknown situation. You don't have to decide anything right now, and it's perfectly fine to change your mind, even at the last second.

 **day 87**

DOCTOR'S ORDERS
Know your options for pain medication early

"Knowing what your options are for pain relief often eases anxiety. There is medication if you need and want it. Your childbirth education class should give you a good overview of pain medication, but it's still important to discuss your options for pain medication with your doctor ahead of time. He or she will be able to give you more specific information on which forms of pain control can be given at each stage of labor."
—K.N.

ADVICE FROM THE TRENCHES
What would a pioneer woman choose?

"I always wonder what the pioneer women that we all refer to when we talk about pain medication in pregnancy would have done if there had been epidurals in their day. I bet you they would have been like, 'Screw being a pioneer, give me that epidural!'"
—Kate, mom to Julia and Ellie

AT THIS POINT
Speaking of pain relief

You may hear that Mother Nature gives pregnant women a hormone that helps them forget the pain of labor. Not true. But she does give us a hefty dose of endorphins (which we can increase through exercise), and this is the closest we get to having a happy hormone. Endorphins help numb the pain and stress of childbirth. After birth, your endorphin levels drop sharply, usually on the same day your S.O. goes back to work, at the exact moment you hear the door close and it hits you: "I'm alone with the baby!"

day 86
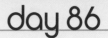

ADVICE FROM THE TRENCHES
Better than hormones

> *"I don't think it's that you forget the pain of childbirth so much as once you have your baby and love her so much, the pain seems a small price to pay, which is why we're willing to go through it again."*
> —April, mom to Daisy and one on the way

HOW TO BREATHE TO RELAX

You'll practice your labor breathing in advance—but right now, you can also use breathing simply to relax and de-stress. Breathing deeply into your belly, rather than high up in your chest area, is very relaxing.

Sit quietly and comfortably with your hand on your belly. If your nose is clear, breathe in through it and out through your mouth. If not, just breathe in and out through your mouth. As you breathe, try to push your belly as far out as you can. Don't allow your breath to stay in your chest—make a conscious effort to move it down. Imagine your breath filling your body and cleansing it. Do this for a few minutes several times a day, and you really will feel better and calmer.

AT THIS POINT
It's time to celebrate the end of your second trimester!

Take your mind off your fear and your aches and pains. Go out and have a big celebratory meal with your S.O. Unlike the end of the last trimester, you're probably having no problem eating. You have come a long way and now have the belly to prove it.

day 85

HOW TO KEEP YOUR PREGNANCY-SPEAK FRESH WHEN YOU FEEL ANYTHING BUT

Did you know that you are a *gravid* female? You're also in a state of *fecundation* right now, thanks to *uberty*, which is a far cry from puberty.

As you begin the third trimester of your countdown (wahoo!), you may be sick of the words *pregnant* or *pregnancy*. Depending on how you're feeling, you may also be sick of *being* pregnant. At least you can keep your pregnancy-speak fresh. Here are some substitutes you may not have thought of for the word *pregnancy*:

abundance, copiousness, evolution, fecundity, feracity, fruitfulness, generative capacity, gravidity, luxuriance, plentifulness, potency, productiveness, productivity, prolificacy, prolificity, ripening, richness, situation, uberty, virility

Now you can tell your boss, "Due to my potency and productivity, not to mention my ongoing prolificacy, the report will be a week late."

AT THIS POINT

How big is your "copious luxuriant of fecundity," anyway?

On your last day of your second trimester, your baby now weighs around 2 pounds, 5 ounces (1 kg), give or take a few ounces.

See, it's not all you!

THE THIRD TRIMESTER

day 84

THE WHOLE TRUTH AND NOTHING BUT
Itchy, bitchy, and huge

Besides the continued growth and development of your baby, the third trimester ultimately serves one purpose: To make you so uncomfortable, *so over it*, so tired, so achy, so bitchy, so itchy, and so freakishly huge, that you will do anything to get the baby out of you, including pushing it out of a place where a tampon once felt *gigantic*. This is Mother Nature's way of inspiring you at the end of your pregnancy, even though we spent the previous eight months thinking, "Okay, how is this going to happen again?"

HURRY UP AND WAIT ALERT
Getting to week 32

Naturally reaching your due date is your ultimate pregnancy countdown moment, but before that wondrous day, there is one major milestone you will hit: week 32. This is a milestone where all pregnant women heave a major sigh of relief. From week 32 on, even if you went into premature labor, your baby will most likely be fine. At week 37, your baby is considered full term. So you're getting there!

AT THIS POINT
You're probably wondering . . .

. . . If 37 weeks is considered full term, why doesn't pregnancy end there? Good question!

Answer: Because pregnancy isn't fair!

Actually, the reason is that although your baby is considered fully developed and viable outside of the womb, she still needs the additional time to add weight and develop her lungs and her immune system further.

day 83

AT THIS POINT
Pregnancy is still enjoyable, at least some of the time

Your third trimester is not exclusively about filling you with the desire to *be done with this pregnancy business*. Yes, you will have lots of aches and pains, but as it begins, you probably still feel pretty good and energetic. There are some wonderful high points: Your baby shower and putting your nursery together. There are some wonderful qualities: You get to complain as much as you want, and each day brings you closer and closer to your ultimate countdown day—your due date—and eventually your beautiful baby.

DOCTOR'S ORDERS
Consider acupuncture

"Acupuncture is a fantastic way to manage stress and alleviate some of your pregnancy aches and pains. Make sure your acupuncturist is familiar with the pregnancy state, because some of their treatments may actually induce labor. Some studies have shown that acupuncture can even help a breech baby turn head-down."
—K.N.

TO-DO LIST
Explore hypnosis

Hypnobirthing isn't just for Hollywood celebs. More and more, hypnobirthing is a technique of self-induced deep relaxation that's effective in many medical procedures, including childbirth. If you want more information, there are many books and CDs now available. Ask at your local bookstore.

day 82

AT THIS POINT
You may have heard about birth plans

Simply put, a birth plan is a written wish list for your birth experience. It details either in a letter or checklist how you want to handle certain situations, like induction or pain medication. Birth plans can be general or highly specific, including details about how you would like the lighting in the room or that you want your birth partner to cut the cord.

TO-DO LIST
Read sample birth plans

Even if you don't intend to write one or decide you don't need one, it's a good idea to actually read some sample birth plans. They'll teach you what to expect during your labor and delivery. Knowing your options can help you discover what may be important to you during the birth process. You may also find new points of discussion to have with your doctor.

ADVICE FROM THE TRENCHES
But you don't know what labor is really like

"I think it's hard to put a plan together for your first delivery. How do you know how you're going to feel? Most moms I know with birth plans implement them for number two."
—Josie, mom to Sarah

DOCTOR'S ORDERS
There are no guarantees

"Among many doctors and nurses, there's a perception that the woman with the most detailed birth plan (i.e., a woman who wants the least amount of medical intervention) ironically always ends up needing a cesarean. This perception, true or not, isn't very fair to women. For a long time, all control was taken away and unnecessary interventions were done to laboring women. A birth plan, regardless of how long it is, is a woman's only way to make her desires clear.

"Approach the birth plan as a way to voice your most important needs or desires, such as, 'Whether I have a cesarean or vaginal birth, if the baby is okay, I would like to nurse him or her as soon as possible,' or 'I would like to avoid pain medication as long as possible, so it is important that I am able to walk around.' Discuss these needs with your partner and your doctor, because you won't always know the doctor or midwife taking care of you in labor."
—K.N.

ADVICE FROM THE TRENCHES
You can still talk!

"I think birth plans are important, but it's also important for women who have never gone through labor to understand that it's not like you become mute, either. Even when you're in pain, you can say, 'No!' or 'Let's wait.'"
—Shelly, mom to Emma

day 80

HOW TO GIVE YOUR BIRTH PLAN A REALITY CHECK

If you do decide to write a birth plan and you're going to deliver in a hospital, don't forget about your labor nurses. They will be on the front line with you. You need to have open-ended communication with them. Consider having your first paragraph of your birth plan be: "I would like to try the items I've outlined here with the understanding that they may not work or be possible. If that is the case (and barring any medical emergencies), I would like a labor nurse to help me understand my options and alternatives and to give me advice."

Having a positive statement like this shows that while you have your own ideas, you're open to communicating with your nurses. You want to show them that you respect their knowledge and experience. And if there is anyone you want on your side during labor, it's your nurse!

ADVICE FROM THE TRENCHES
A very simple birth plan

"My birth plan is short and simple: I plan to be in as little pain as possible."
—Rosemary, forty-five days to go

TO-DO LIST
Talk to your birth partner about your wishes

If you don't feel a birthing plan is a necessity, but you have strong feelings about pain medication or how long you're willing to labor before being induced, then talk to your birth partner. Whether this person is your husband or a friend, he or she will help you communicate to your nurses what you would like to happen during labor.

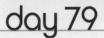

ADVICE FROM THE TRENCHES
Three positive experiences

"I have three babies, and I think the reason I had a positive experience each time is that I had a good relationship and open communication with my doctor."
—Allison, mom to Katie, Abby, Johnny, and one on the way

AT THIS POINT
Know there's no failure

The most important thing about a birth plan is to stay flexible. We can imagine how our labor will go, and the opposite will happen. Your baby may be breech. Your baby may develop a health issue. Your labor may drag on for three days. If your baby's heartbeat suddenly drops and you need an emergency C-section, you will not have control.

You don't know what your labor and delivery are going to be like, even if you've had three children already. Each baby and each birth is unique.

The bottom line: No mom who eventually leaves the hospital with a baby has failed!

THE WHOLE TRUTH AND NOTHING BUT
Mother Nature must have adopted

The more you think about labor and childbirth during this trimester, the more convinced you'll become that Mother Nature must have adopted. She must not have experienced this firsthand—why else would she make pregnancy like this?!?

day 78

TO-DO LIST
Ask your doctor what to expect

When it comes to labor and delivery, so much is out of your control, but you can maintain a sense of emotional control by asking questions about routine procedures, such as induction, and knowing what to realistically expect. Make sure you talk to your doctor about these and any other procedures you may go through:

* **Will I be shaved?** More and more doctors do not require that you be shaved, although in some cases, if you have a C-section, you may be shaved.

* **What is your policy on induction if my "water" breaks?** Many doctors, fearing infection, will induce within twenty-four hours of rupture.

* **What is your policy on fetal monitoring?** Some women prefer not to be restricted in movement during active labor, and this can be difficult with constant fetal monitoring.

* **Will I be allowed to eat?** Most doctors want you to have an empty stomach because your digestion doesn't work well during labor. Some allow hard candy and ice chips.

* **Besides an epidural, what pain-relieving medications are available to me?** Can I get a "walking" epidural? (This is a newer type that allows you to still feel and move your legs.) What are the possible side effects of each drug?

* **If I need a C-section, what are the restrictions during the procedure?** Will my birthing partner have to leave the room? For details on C-sections, see Days 28 to 22.

day 77

AT THIS POINT
You're 29 weeks pregnant!

Around now, your doctor or midwife will probably start seeing you every two weeks to check you and your baby.

And speaking of your baby, she's just over 16^1/$_2$ inches (about 42 cm) long from head to toe. She weighs about 2 pounds, 4 ounces (1 kg). Over the next three months, your baby will more than triple her weight. By the end of a full-term pregnancy, the average weight of a baby born in the United States is 7^1/$_2$ pounds (3.4 kg).

DOCTOR'S ORDERS
How we determine your baby's weight

"Here's something that might surprise you. Despite all of our amazing technology, doctors estimate your baby's weight in the third trimester by palpating your abdomen and comparing the fetal size to a five-pound bag of sugar. Believe it or not, obstetrical residents hone this skill by practicing on laboring patients. When the baby is born, they get to see if they were right."
—K.N.

day 76

THE WHOLE TRUTH AND NOTHING BUT

How much bigger are you going to get?

On an average, you might expect to put on another pound (450 g) a week. Remember, some of this will be fluid. But if you do the math and find that you are going over 40 pounds, talk to your doctor to make sure you both feel okay about it.

AT THIS POINT

Learn how to squat

While it's a good idea to exercise for as long as you can, if you just don't feel good enough for cardio, you can still do some exercises, like squatting, to prepare for labor. Squatting during delivery—with assistance—opens your pelvis even wider so the baby has more room to move down into the birth canal. Using a wall for support is a great way to practice at home. Simply stand with your back flat against a wall with your feet shoulder-width apart. Slide your back down the wall until you're in a position similar to sitting on a chair. Lightly rest your hands on your thighs and count to three. Slide back up. Repeat, gradually working yourself up to 5 to 10 repetitions. Once you build up your strength, you can try it without the wall, but always have a doorway or sturdy chair nearby for support if you get wobbly. You can even lower yourself onto a low stool so it's easier to get up.

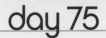

day 75

HURRY UP AND WAIT ALERT
A third trimester perk!

Finally, a fun wait in Pregnancy Land. You'll be having a baby shower soon. Baby gear and cake . . . no wonder you're excited. Most moms-to-be have a shower in their third trimester, usually a month or two before their due date.

TO-DO LIST
Brush up on your baby shower etiquette

According to Miss Manners, baby showers should not be thrown by family members because it's considered rude to ask for presents for someone you're related to. It might appear like a gift grab, and apparently Miss Manners feels it's preferable to have a friend stage the gift grab. In these more socially relaxed times, many women choose to follow newer and more relaxed etiquette guidelines. Who cares who throws the baby shower, as long as you're having a good time?

THE WHOLE TRUTH AND NOTHING BUT
You may feel superstitious

Many women feel funny about having a baby shower before the baby arrives, either because of cultural beliefs or because, well, some just feel like they're jinxing things. If you feel this way, have your shower after your baby is born. A bonus to an after-birth baby shower: If you're not breastfeeding, you can have a glass of spiked sherbet punch. If you are breastfeeding, you get to have two pieces of cake, no questions asked. Plus, you'll know what items you still need by then.

HOW TO KEEP THE PEACE

Unless it's strictly a "girlfriends only" event, if you have more than one baby shower, invite both your mother and mother-in-law to each one. Feelings get hurt!

TO-DO LIST
Buy a stack of index cards

Here's a great way to let all the women in the room have their chance to give you their best advice on childbirth and newborn care—maybe it will get it out of their systems so you can eat in peace.

Before you open your gifts, ask your guests to please write down their advice. Hand out the index cards and pens and then put a friend in charge of collecting them. You may get some great tips. You can make these into a keepsake book or add these cards to your baby scrapbook.

ADVICE FROM THE TRENCHES
Keep it short

"Having been given a baby shower and having thrown one, my advice is to ask your shower-giver to keep it short and simple. Unlike your bridal shower, baby showers are exhausting, especially toward the end of your third trimester. For my sister's baby shower, we had people eat as soon as everyone had arrived, and then she opened gifts while the guests ate. (She ate beforehand.) The whole thing took two hours from start to finish, and I think that's about as long as anyone wants to be hanging out at a baby shower."
—Michelle, mom to Elizabeth

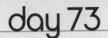

day 73

HOW TO REGISTER FOR YOUR BABY SHOWER

As you have probably already discovered, it costs a small fortune to properly equip your home, nursery, car, playroom, kitchen, bathroom, and bedroom with the latest baby gear and gadgets.

Hurray for baby showers and registries that allow you to get what you really want! Here are four guidelines to keep in mind when you register:

1. **Go with a list or a plan.** If you don't have a clear idea of what you want, you may go berserk once you get in the store. Before you register, scope out what you want online or take a stroll through some stores a day or two before the official registering event.

2. **Think about what you really need now.** You can certainly register for a high chair or feeding chair, but you're not going to need one until further down the road. Same goes for the exersaucer—babies can't use these until they can hold their heads up.

3. **Take along another mom for expert advice and guidance on gadgets and must-haves.**

4. **Make sure that the person throwing your shower knows where you're registered, so the name of the store can be communicated to guests.**

ADVICE FROM THE TRENCHES

No surprises, please!

"I think surprise baby showers are a bad idea. Do you really want to scare a pregnant woman one month before her due date?"
—Karen, mom to Jenna

day 72

HOW TO OPEN BABY SHOWER GIFTS

Yes, you've been to a hundred baby showers, but did you ever actually pay attention to the gift-opening? Didn't think so. Here are the guidelines.

1. You have to hold everything up so everyone can go: "Aww" and "Ohh."

2. When you get a duplicate gift, say: "Great, I wanted another one to have at my sister's/mother's/mother-in-law's house."

3. Start opening gifts as soon as possible. Unlike your bridal shower, you are probably going to be wiped out and exhausted—it's a lot harder when pregnant, so make sure you have plenty of time.

4. Ask someone to please make sure they're writing everything down for you— remember, you have a pregnancy-impaired brain.

5. You can hold up a gift, like a baby tub, and say, "My husband will get a lot of use out of this, ha, ha," but everyone in the room will know the joke's on you.

6. Cut the cake first. That way, you'll have the strength to go on.

TO-DO LIST
Buy a hostess gift

It might not be technically required to give the person/people who throw you a shower a gift, but it's a nice gesture. For a perfect gift that's thoughtful and affordable, you can't beat a bouquet of flowers. You can send them before or after the big event, or you can simply bring them with you. (Miss Manners will be proud.)

THE WHOLE TRUTH AND NOTHING BUT
You will be ambushed!

You know how you've been assaulted these last several weeks by people who want to pet your belly, tell you epidural failure stories, or who just want to regale you with tales of babies who refuse to sleep for three months straight?

Well, guess what? Your baby shower is potentially a belly-petting and horror-story fest. Your best strategy: Have a friend or relative who can run interference for you when Aunt Betty gets you in a corner, or if talk turns to how many stitches she had with each of her giant children.

TO-DO LIST
Save a piece of cake

Here's a really sweet idea: Take a piece of your shower cake and put it in the freezer. At your baby's first birthday, thaw it out, put a candle in it, and eat it to celebrate your baby's wonderful occasion—her first year of life.

ADVICE FROM THE TRENCHES
You never know what will come in handy

"I got a baby wipe warmer at my shower. At the time I thought it was a waste and almost returned it. But now, I find that a nice warm wipe in the middle of the night makes for less crying."
—Patty, mom to Sean and Max

day 70

AT THIS POINT
What's happening with your baby?

Your baby is growing taller by the day. This week, she weighs almost 3 pounds (1.4 kg). Next time you're at the grocery store, put a cantaloupe on the scale. That will give you a good idea of what three pounds weigh. She measures more than 17 inches (38 cm) long from head to toe.

If you've had your childbirth education class, you've been practicing your breathing techniques—and so is your baby. Even though she's still breathing amniotic fluid, she's mimicking the movements of breathing so she'll be ready for her big day. Lungs continue to develop through the third trimester. At this point, your baby may even get the hiccups—but it's nothing to worry about. This can sometimes be seen on ultrasound, and it's a sign of fetal well-being.

DOCTOR'S ORDERS
Know when swelling is not okay

"Swelling in your legs and feet is common and normal and is usually not a problem unless it involves your hands and face. If you are experiencing high blood pressure and protein in your urine in addition to the swelling, this could be a sign of preeclampsia—a disorder that occurs only in pregnancy. The cause of preeclampsia is unknown and can be dangerous if it goes undetected. If you are diagnosed with it, your doctor will watch you very closely and deliver you early if things worsen. The majority of the time baby and mommy have a very healthy outcome."
—K.N.

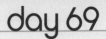
THE WHOLE TRUTH AND NOTHING BUT
The gadget vortex

Remember how you got obsessed, really obsessed, about all the details of your wedding? That was the bridal vortex.

You're entering a far more obsessive vortex now—the gadget and baby gear vortex. Unlike your wedding, which ended, the gadget vortex doesn't. As your child grows, he'll require more gadgets, and there's no getting out once you're sucked in. And because most of these gadgets will keep your child sleeping, germ-free, comfy, warm, snuggled, and monitored, you will obsess that you are getting the best ones, or at least the best ones that you can afford. Just do your best and know that every parent goes through this, too.

ADVICE FROM THE TRENCHES
Never give up on a gadget

"Here is the most important thing to understand about baby gadgets like swings, vibrating seats, exersaucers, and all the rest—if you put your child in one and she screams, don't give up. Babies change weekly on what they like and don't like. My advice: Buy or borrow as much as you can and try them all. Something will work!"
—Clare, mom to Annie and Grace

TO-DO LIST
Start hoarding batteries now

Just about every baby item these days—from hanging crib toys to baby seats—will vibrate, light up, talk, buzz, beep, and/or play music. You will not believe how many batteries babyhood requires. And not just one size—you will need all sizes. Start stocking up now.

THE WHOLE TRUTH AND NOTHING BUT
Ga-ga for gadgets

There are so many "must-have" baby gear items, it's mind-boggling. But here's the bottom line about gear and gadgets for the budget- or space-conscious: You don't really *need* most of them. *Wanting* is a whole different story. All you really need right away—besides basics like diapers, onesies, and blankets—is a car seat and a bassinette. It's okay to take a wait-and-see-what-we'll-need approach.

HOW TO KEEP YOUR PERSPECTIVE

As the writer Dave Barry reminds us, we didn't always have all of this baby stuff:

"When I was born, during the presidency of James K. Polk, we babies did not require a lot of equipment. We had our blanket, and that was pretty much it. . . . If we were lucky, we'd have a rattle, which we would obtain by catching an actual rattlesnake with our tiny bare hands. Also in those days, we changed our own diapers."

ADVICE FROM THE TRENCHES
Baby monitors

"Always remember: When your baby monitor is on, someone nearby with their baby monitor on could be hearing every word you're saying in your own house!"
—Tracy, mom to Jake, Paul, and Shannon

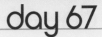

TO-DO LIST
Buy a combo infant car seat/stroller

Let's imagine a worst-case scenario: You're having a baby soon, money is tight, your living space is small, and you and your S.O. are only children of only children. On top of all that, you've just moved, so you don't have any friends to buy you gifts. What's the one item that you must buy?

ANSWER: A good stroller with a built-in infant car seat. Here's why:

* **Necessity:** You need the infant car seat, anyway. You *will* actually be leaving your house with your baby.

* **Convenience:** Just pop them from the carrier in the stroller to the car.

* **Versatility:** Babies often sleep in their car seats. And in a pinch, a car seat can also be used to soothe a baby to sleep by rocking it gently back and forth. Or, you can sit down and move the stroller back and forth. (Just don't do this near stairs!)

ADVICE FROM THE TRENCHES
Do what works!

"Our daughter would only sleep in her car seat. She hated sleeping flat on her back and propped on her side. We think that she liked to be elevated. So we did what any sleep-deprived parents would do—we put her car seat in her crib, and we all got some sleep!"
—Susan, mom to Esther and Sophie

 **day 66**

ADVICE FROM THE TRENCHES
Baby bath towels

"The little baby towels with a hood that you can buy are basically worthless; they're too small and not absorbent. I make my own: I take a regular bath towel and sew a terrycloth hood in the middle. In fact, I make them as baby gifts for friends, and they love them."

—Bethany, mom to Milo and Meena

HOW TO MAKE SURE THE ITEMS YOU'RE BUYING ARE SAFE

The U.S. Consumer Product Safety Commission's (CPSC) Web site (http://search.cpsc.gov) is a must-visit for cautious parents-to-be. The CPSC ensures the safety of consumer products available in the United States, including products for babies. They have many free publications available about baby products, safety guidelines, and product recalls.

Another great Web-based organization, Child Safety Experts (www.childsafetyexperts.com), provides free guidance, product recommendations, and links for making smart decisions on car seats and other important safety equipment.

THE WHOLE TRUTH AND NOTHING BUT
Are your hand-me-downs safe?

It's really great to get hand-me-down baby items, like swings and strollers. But you still need to visit the CPSC Web site and make sure the product wasn't recalled or isn't so old that it doesn't have the right safety features.

AT THIS POINT
You're wondering if all that swinging is really safe

Though it might make you dizzy, babies love to swing, sometimes for hours. According to the Mayo Clinic, "With proper supervision, baby swings are appropriate for babies from birth to about age nine months, or until they reach a weight of 25 pounds (11.3 kg). The back-and-forth motion of the swing may soothe a crying baby or help a newborn fall asleep. Many pediatricians recommend swings to parents of colicky babies. This motion isn't violent enough to harm an infant's brain."

TO-DO LIST
Start your baby's library

Hopefully, you'll get some good books as gifts, but if you don't, start building your baby's library now. Board books are a good, indestructible choice for babies who will eventually tear and chew. You can start reading to your baby when he's a few months old. Even if he doesn't understand, it's a nice way to establish a bedtime routine. Besides, you'll love these books so much, you'll read them just because you enjoy them:

Goodnight Moon, by Margaret Wise Brown

Guess How Much I Love You, by Sam McBratney

The Very Hungry Caterpillar, by Eric Carle

Brown Bear, Brown Bear, What Do You See?, by Bill Martin Jr.

Good Night, Gorilla, by Peggy Rathmann

day 64

THE WHOLE TRUTH AND NOTHING BUT
Babies spend lots of time in jammies

Though you may be tempted to buy lots of cute little outfits or even to register for them, *don't*. As you'll discover in another sixty-four days or so, babies are poop and spit-up machines. You don't need one hundred cute outfits in the 0–3 size with poop and vomit on them. You need one hundred onesies—the little one-piece jammies babies hang out in all day. The only time you'll be dressing up your 0–3-month-old baby is for holidays and for doctor visits so your pediatrician doesn't think you're the kind of mom who lets her kid hang out in jammies all day.

HOW TO FIND REALLY COOL BABY CLOTHES

Okay, you're only human. You have to splurge on at least one (or two) really cool baby outfits. If you're looking beyond the pink or blue traditional clothing scene, the Web is a great place to find cool and alternative baby clothes. Check out:

www.luckylildevil.com. This is a fun place to find punk and Goth clothes for babies. What baby girl doesn't look awesome in a punk kilt at three months?

http://store.kidbean.com. This is the place to find organic clothes and baby kimonos.

ADVICE FROM THE TRENCHES
Buy the socks built in

"If you see baby pants with built-in socks, buy three pairs because they're hard to find—probably because moms are buying all of them. Baby socks never stay on feet, and it will drive you nuts."
—Renee, mom to Steven and Anderson

31 Weeks Pregnant!

day 63

AT THIS POINT
What's happening with your baby?

At week 31, your baby weighs about 3 pounds, 5 ounces (1.5 kg) and measures approximately 18 inches (46 cm) from head to toe.

Your baby's central nervous system is controlling more of her bodily functions now. If your baby is exposed to bright light, her irises will dilate, even in utero.

THE WHOLE TRUTH AND NOTHING BUT
Deep breathing, all right!

As you put on more weight, you may start to change from pink to red—that's because your body may be rubbing and itching in ways that you're not used to. You may feel very breathless, and your heart may pound from a walk up the stairs. You might be worrying that if you're not getting air, how is your baby? But she's fine. She gets all the oxygen she needs from the placenta.

TO-DO LIST
Learn about the *vernix caseosa*

Vernix caseosa (vur-niks ka-SEE-oh-sa) is one pregnancy term that actually sounds nicer than what it is: a fatty, cheese-like, white substance that now coats your baby's entire body. This coating protects her skin during its long submersion in amniotic fluid. This slick coating will also help her journey down the birth canal— so hopefully she has lots of it! She may be born with it on her skin, which illustrates yet another of the profound differences between TV newborns and real ones.

day 62

HOW TO BOND WITH YOUR S.O.

Setting up the baby's room is so much fun. It is the only room in your house that your S.O. won't complain about painting or going furniture shopping for. Work it! Baby room shopping is also the only time when you won't mind going to Home Depot or the paint store, so this is a major bonding opportunity for you and your S.O.

TO-DO LIST
Buy extra fire alarms

While you're out shopping for paint and window treatments, this is the perfect time to make sure you have enough fire alarms in your home. You'll need at least one smoke detector on every floor, placed outside the bedrooms, either on the ceiling or six to twelve inches (15.2–30.4 cm) below the ceiling on the wall. Be sure to check the batteries every year (your child's birthday is an easy anniversary to remember). Also, many new parents will put smoke alarms both inside and outside a baby's room—just in case.

ADVICE FROM THE TRENCHES
You will love visiting your baby's room

"After we finished the baby's room, I would gravitate there all the time. Several times a day, I would find myself sitting in the rocker, looking around and visualizing this amazing life I had ahead of me. It's a very fun time. Try to get it done early so you can enjoy it before all hell breaks loose!"
—Marianne, mom to Patrick and Andy

THE WHOLE TRUTH AND NOTHING BUT
Bumper set scam

Those matching crib and bumper sets—bumpers, mobile, crib skirt, sheet, quilt, hamper, hanging diaper bag—that baby stores sell are so darn cute, and there are so many to choose from. But before you shell out for a whole matching set, you should know that almost no one uses the hanging diaper bag—it's just easier to stack diapers—and for safety reasons, you can't use the quilt in the crib for about a year. All you really need are the bumpers, two or three crib sheets, and a mobile.

HOW TO USE YOUR ADORABLE QUILT

If you do buy a whole crib set complete with a quilt, don't keep the quilt in a closet. Get some double-sided Velcro and use it as an adorable wall hanging in your baby's room. Later, when it gets used as an actual blanket, you'll have to find something to replace it, but in the meantime, it won't go to waste.

ADVICE FROM THE TRENCHES
Nursery madness

"The truth is that your first baby gets this beautiful nursery, and by the time you have a third, that poor baby gets put in the walk-in closet for a year."
—Esther, mom to Bryant, Dashiel, and Katherine

day 60

THE WHOLE TRUTH AND NOTHING BUT

Does music really calm babies?

Just about every baby product these days seems to play music. Is this just a marketing ploy? Does music really calm babies?

According to scientists, the answer is yes. *Neonatal Network: The Journal of Neonatal Nursing* reported that "soothing music with a flowing, lyrical, simple harmony, soft tone color, and easy rhythm (about 60 to 80 beats per minute) can help to stimulate the relaxation response."

HOW TO RECREATE YOUR WOMB SOUNDS

If music works to calm babies, why not take it one step further? Dr. Fred J. Schwartz of Piedmont Hospital in Atlanta, Georgia, discovered that music mixed with womb sounds—whooshing blood and mom's heartbeat—soothed fussy babies. Even parents report that they are soothed by the sounds. There are numerous CDs on the market that combine music with simulated womb sounds.

ADVICE FROM THE TRENCHES

A really simple way to soothe your baby

"Call me old-fashioned, but I think the best way to get a baby to sleep is to lay him on your chest so he can feel your heartbeat and breathing. That worked for me."
—Josie, mom to Sarah

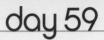

AT THIS POINT
He's not moving as much!

By now, your baby is getting bigger and his living space is getting smaller. This means the quality of your baby's fetal activity may change and may cause you to worry. All pregnant women go through this worry. Sharp, hard jabs may now turn into more rolling motions.

DOCTOR'S ORDERS
Do kick counts

"A good way to keep track of your baby's movement is to do fetal kick counts. Pick a time of day that your baby is usually active, and count how long it takes the baby to move ten times. It should take thirty to sixty minutes. Then every day around that time, make sure he takes approximately the same amount of time. This is a way to ensure your baby is doing his or her regular activity. Sometimes you can catch babies in a twenty- to thirty-minute sleep cycle. If this happens, get up, walk around, eat something, and try again. It is a good idea to do this during the day so that if there is any question of how active the baby is, you can call your doctor. When it comes to fetal movement, your baby should still be active at his or her usual times. Never hesitate to call your doctor if you are ever concerned."
—K.N.

THE WHOLE TRUTH AND NOTHING BUT
Bed rest is challenging

If for whatever reason you end up on bed rest, you are going to need quite a few gadgets for *yourself*—portable phone, TV with DVD player, a lot of friends to visit, and, most importantly, computer access to make it through the rest of your countdown. Or you can always take a low-tech approach and learn how to knit or crochet. You can make your baby's first blanket.

DOCTOR'S ORDERS
Why you may need bed rest

"There are several situations where your doctor may prescribe bed rest, such as pregnancy-induced hypertension, preeclampsia, or preterm labor. The good news about preterm labor is if you made it to week 37, you can get out of bed for the first time. If, however, your blood pressure is going up or if you have swelling in your hands and face and protein in your urine, you will need to rest as much as possible until you go into labor. If you are on bed rest, try to look at it as your last chance to lie in bed and do absolutely nothing, because it will be!"
—K.N.

TO-DO LIST
Get a lot of support

If you're on bed rest, you'll definitely want to visit www.sidelines.org. Sidelines is an organization that supports high-risk pregnant women. You can get tons of information and even a "phone buddy" to help you through your difficult and emotional situation.

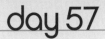

HOW TO CELEBRATE YOUR BELLINESS

Consider a romantic dinner with your S.O. and then a belly cast session.

A what? Technically, it's really a belly/breast cast because you get the mold of your whole torso. You and your S.O. apply wet plaster strips to your body. (This could be the closet thing you get to sex for a while.) When it sets and then is removed, there's your big belly and big breasts preserved for years to come. Some moms even paint and decorate them. Somewhere, some proud mom probably has hers hanging in her living room, but where you put your belly cast is up to you. Belly cast kits are safe and are available from many maternity stores.

AT THIS POINT
Plan for a "baby fire drill" with your S.O.

You plan so much for your baby, but don't forget to plan with your S.O., too. Your relationship will go through yet another major readjustment period (read: you may hate each other again for a while).

A new baby may be a welcome addition, but he's going to be a stressful one, too. It can be helpful and calming to have a plan in place for when the baby arrives and all hell breaks loose. Talk about how you want to handle the baby duty when your S.O. comes home from work. Will you have an immediate hand-off? (Yes!) Who does household chores? (He will!) If you're bottle-feeding, will you split the duty in nightly shifts? (You better believe it!) For the first few weeks, can he come home for lunch? Early from work? (Better yet, just don't let him leave at all!)

day 56

HOW TO VISUALIZE YOUR BABY

From head to toe, your baby is about 18 1/2 inches (47 cm) long. This explains why you feel like there's a foot up around your ribcage. There probably *is* a foot or another body part in your ribcage. Your baby weighs around 4 pounds (1.8 kg), though to you it probably feels like 10 pounds (4.5 kg).

HURRY UP AND WAIT ALERT

Will this ever end?

Your baby is running out of room, and you're running out of patience. (*Big sigh*). You still have 56 days to go—or more. The end of your third trimester is when life in Pregnancy Land can get really hard again. You may still be working and anxiously awaiting your maternity leave. You may now have shooting pains down your legs during the day and bad leg cramps at night. Many women experience fatigue and PMS-like symptoms. To make matters worse, sleeping comfortably is difficult, if not impossible. By now, your S.O. is either in the guest room, on the couch, or being smothered by your boyfriend Bob, the full body pillow, and a host of other pillows.

ADVICE FROM THE TRENCHES

Pregnancy is really 10 months!

"Why does everyone say that pregnancy is 9 months when it's really 10? Do the math! Week 32 is your eighth month, but you still have around 60 days to go—that's two more months!"

—Serena, mom to Jason

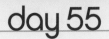

day 55

TO-DO LIST
Join a warehouse club

You know you've entered a much less cool era of your life when you join a wholesale shopping club. Even if you don't want food by the carton, the price of membership will pay for itself in savings on diapers and other baby supplies. You can also get great deals on brand-name baby clothing. They know how to lure moms and dads in to shop—deep discounts on baby stuff.

ADVICE FROM THE TRENCHES
Don't be a diaper snob

"Don't be afraid to try the store brand diapers, which are a lot cheaper. I used to do the store brand for daytime and the premium brand just for bedtime. You'll save a lot of money this way."
—Lucy, mom to Annabelle and Christina

THE WHOLE TRUTH AND NOTHING BUT
Who turned on the cappuccino machine?

You'll feed and change your little darling and then in twenty minutes you'll hear a curious sputter and gurgle. You'll say, "Who turned on the cappuccino machine?" Then you'll realize there is no cappuccino machine; it's your baby—*again*.

According to the University of Missouri's Children, Youth, and Family Consortium, the average baby is diapered *seven thousand* times before she's potty trained. Newborns need to be changed around *ten* times a day. After six weeks to a month, that number usually goes down to around seven times a day, which (by that point) feels like a diaper vacation.

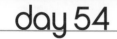

day 54

TO-DO LIST
Talk to your S.O. about what support he may need

Though some S.O.s would like to have a painkiller during *your* labor, that's not going to happen. So what can they have to help them through this exciting and scary process?

One possibility is to include your best girlfriend, mom, or sister in the labor room. It's not that you must have a third party and another woman present, but if you're in the throes of a long labor, another person can give you additional support so your S.O. can take a break. Just because you can't eat while in labor doesn't mean he can't sneak to the cafeteria while you're napping in the bliss of epiduralness. But be sure to ask your S.O. if this extra presence will make him feel less involved or necessary.

Also, encourage your S.O. to attend a doctor visit soon if he has questions. He may be worried that something will happen to you or the baby, or that he'll faint or do something stupid.

DOCTOR'S ORDERS
Don't buy into the fainting dad myth

"Most dads do great in the delivery room. Many want to see everything and be an active participant. But Dads, if you are at all squeamish, don't try to be stoic. If you feel faint, let the nurse know and sit right down. Only one person gets to be the patient. Most partners have the hardest time watching their wives in pain. Once their wives have their epidurals, Dads feel much better too."
—K.N.

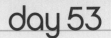

day 53

AT THIS POINT
You may want to consider hiring help

You can hire a certified labor doula to be with you and your partner through the whole labor experience at the hospital. This can be an especially important option for moms who are going at it alone or who may have a spouse who knows he will be away at the time of birth (not because he wants to!).

A doula is professionally trained to help with labor, your recovery, newborn care, and breastfeeding.

THE WHOLE TRUTH AND NOTHING BUT
But you can barely afford more underwear!

A labor doula can be expensive. If you have any money budgeted for a doula, you may feel that the time you will need her help is after the baby arrives. (And you may be right.)

HOW TO START SAVING MONEY NOW

* **Consider refinancing your mortgage.** Yes, it's a pain, but you could save several hundred dollars a month.

* **Cut back on entertainment.** Once your baby is born, you'll have dozens of hours of entertainment just staring at him. Who needs digital cable? And those four magazine subscriptions? Forget it. You will not have time to read four magazines. Maybe one, if your baby is a good napper.

* **Start cutting your own grass.** Once the baby is born, your S.O. will actually love getting out to cut the grass that you used to pay someone else to cut. It may be the closest thing he gets to playing golf for several months.

* **Start living off of your S.O.'s income now.** Bank or pay off debts with yours.

Maybe a doula is doable after all!

HOW TO GET UNSTUCK ABOUT THE NAME

Bailey? Bridget? Bernadette? Bettinna? Beyonce? Boston? Becky? Beatrice? Bethany? BLAHHHHHH!

Some couples struggle with their baby name until the last second. If you're one of those name-stuck couples, don't panic, you still have 52 days in your countdown to get unstuck.

Have you thought about a middle name? A middle name can solve a lot of problems. If a relative really wants your baby to have his or her name, maybe you can hide it in the middle. You can even give your baby two middle names if you have two potentially unhappy relatives.

If your S.O. has a strong opinion about your baby name, then maybe the solution is for you to get middle naming rights. A lot of people use mom's maiden name for the baby's middle name.

AT THIS POINT
Maybe someone else should name your baby

If you are truly at an impasse with your S.O. about your baby's name, or you simply can't make up your mind, you can submit your short list of names to names@iparenting.com, and they'll put them to a vote on the *Pregnancy Today* Web site. Just agree ahead of time that whatever name is chosen is the one you'll go with.

HOW TO DEAL WITH YOUR UNREASONABLE, UNCARING, UNSYMPATHETIC S.O.

Not only is he being a first class pain about baby names, you may find that your S.O. is making comments about the amount of food you're eating, weight you're gaining, or exercise he wishes you were doing. Even though you probably hate him for it, try to see his side of things. You're literally growing before his eyes. Your underwear is now bigger than his. While your pregnancy is exciting for him, it has to be scary to see his partner go up four sizes.

AT THIS POINT
Your rose-colored glasses are off, too!

At least you will one day give birth and decrease in size and appetite. Your S.O., on the other hand, will still be the same person annoying you. You probably have a list of behaviors that he'll have to stop once the baby arrives. For starters: No more yelling at other drivers, burping at the dinner table, throwing underwear on the floor, and laying around on Sunday watching football. That's gotta stop!

THE WHOLE TRUTH AND NOTHING BUT
Yep, you're in your third trimester, all right

You were so happy for a while! But now, you're both getting nervous as your countdown day draws nearer and nearer. Naturally, there's going to be tension.

In other words, welcome to the third trimester relationship strain. It ain't pretty, but all pregnant couples go through it, and most get over it at least by the time the baby starts preschool. (Just kidding. It can take several weeks to a few months to get your relationship groove back, but it *will* come back.)

# day 50

HOW TO GET JOME JIZE PERJPECTIVE

You know that number on the scale cannot possibly be all you! You're right. Here's a typical weight breakdown for the end of your pregnancy:

* 7 to 9 pounds (3–4 kg) of baby

* 2 pounds (900 g) of placenta

* 4 to 5 pounds (1.8–2.2 kg) of increased blood volume

* 2 pounds (900 g) of fundus

* 3 to 4 pounds (1.3–1.8 kg) of fluid in maternal tissue (this is the swelling you see in your ankles)

* 1 to 2 pounds (450–900 g) of breast enlargement

Any remaining pounds are a general deposit of fat required by the body for breastfeeding and energy stores—e.g., your big behind and giant feet!

TO-DO LIJT
Squeeze when you sneeze

Even if you've been doing your kegels, you may still feel the need to squeeze your pelvic muscles when you sneeze. At this stage of pregnancy, it's dangerous to even laugh. Wearing a pad and traveling with an extra pair of underwear and a plastic bag can be helpful. This often gets worse over the course of the next weeks and may not let up until a few months after your baby is born. Though truthfully, some find that a little bit of a leak is, well, permanent upon sneezing.

AT THIJ POINT
You've heard the one about . . .

. . . the woman who didn't know she was pregnant until she fell on the floor of the grocery store/elevator/rest room/restaurant and gave birth.

Yeah. Right.

AT THIS POINT
You're 33 weeks pregnant!

With less than 2 months to go, your baby weighs about 4.4 pounds (2 kg) and is almost 19 inches (48 cm) long. All of her bones are still hardening, except for her skull, which remains soft and pliable and will not completely join, enabling her to journey through the birth canal.

HOW TO CLEAN YOUR HOUSE

Just surrender to your nesting instinct. "Nesting"—the desire to clean, redo, and renew one's home—is real. Nesting is a primal instinct among all pregnant animals. It often hits the human ones during the third trimester. (In fact, a strong nesting urge at your due date week can even signal the onset of labor.)

So just as a bird prepares her nest, you're preparing your "nest" or nursery and home for the arrival of your baby.

Though you'll have bouts of fatigue, you're also going to have bouts of energy and a desire to sterilize your walls and doorknobs, rearrange the furniture, or make curtains, even though you have never sewn in your life. Go for it! You may never have this impulse again.

TO-DO LIST
Start freezing food

While you're nesting, make and freeze food. If you're not in the mood to cook, and you're still in the pre-baby take-out mode, order extra and freeze it. Once the baby arrives, and your expenses increase, you don't have to feel guilty for splurging for take-out—again!

day 48

TO-DO LIST
Buy a crock pot

The crock pot must have been invented by a new mom. Crock pots allow you to get dinner preparation over early in the day, and this is especially important with babies who fuss in the late afternoon/early evening (which is to say, all babies). Get at least a three-quart (2.8-liter) cooker—any smaller doesn't allow for leftovers. Start experimenting with it now. When you have a newborn baby you won't have the time or energy to learn how to use it.

ADVICE FROM THE TRENCHES
Getting dinner made

"When my son was a newborn, I would prepare—chop, slice, and mix—as much of dinner as I could first thing in the morning while my husband was still around and the baby was calm. Even a simple stir-fry can overwhelm you at 5:00 P.M., when there's a crying baby in the house."
—Margaret, mom to Shane and Colleen

HOW TO MAKE DIAPER WIPES

If you're nesting and looking for a project, make and store some of your own baby wipes in an airtight container. Baby wipes are something you will always be running out of and always need. Plus, unlike the store-bought kinds, they don't cause rashes or have heavy perfume.

* 2 teaspoons (10 ml) baby wash
* 2 teaspoons (10 ml) baby oil
* 2 cups (475 ml) hot water
* 1 roll of paper towels, cut in half, cardboard removed

Mix baby wash, baby oil, and water in a large airtight plastic container and add half a roll of paper towels. Pull up from the center. Store with lid on to retain moisture.

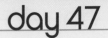

day 47

AT THIS POINT

What does your house look like?

Clean! Maybe even sterilized! (However, let your S.O. clean the oven because strong chemical cleaners and bleach have fumes that are not good for you and baby.)

By now, you may even have a few baby books with titles like *How to Bring Your Baby Home Without Injuring Her* and *I Love You Baby, but Go to Sleep*.

It's never to soon to start reading up on how to care for newborns and how to get them to sleep.

HOW TO GET A BABY TO SLEEP

As you'll discover, there is a whole industry designed around getting your baby to sleep—gadgets, books, and many theories offered by professionals and laypeople alike.

According to Marc Weissbluth, M.D., sleep specialist and author of *Healthy Sleep Habits, Happy Child*, babies are not capable of organizing sleep patterns until they're at least four months old. This means you can't even attempt to get a baby on a schedule until he's four months—older if he was a preemie.

This is one of the reasons why going back to work at three months can be tremendously difficult. You still may have no idea when you're going to get any sleep.

But once your baby is four months old, Weissbluth's book and the equally popular book by sleep expert Richard Ferber, M.D., *Solve Your Child's Sleep Problem*, will be a total revelation to sleepy parents.

day 46

ADVICE FROM THE TRENCHES
It can't stay that bad . . .

"Most couples I know totally panic in the first weeks and even months of bringing a baby home. I tell them what my sister told me: 'If it didn't eventually get a whole lot easier at some point soon, no one would ever have more than one. You would be too tired and too afraid to have sex ever again."
—Mary Beth, mom to Trevor and Justin

AT THIS POINT
What's happening (or not happening) with your sex life

The bigger you get belly-wise, the harder it can be to have sex. If your baby "drops" early, penetration may be unpleasant and even painful. Though orgasms have always triggered contractions, it's scarier when you're bigger. But as long as they don't increase in intensity or frequency before week 37, you're safe. Even though sex is still safe, it can be unnerving. You may be so preoccupied with the baby that it's the last thing on your mind.

THE WHOLE TRUTH AND NOTHING BUT
Erotic dreams may be all you need

Though your sex life may slow down by the end of this trimester, here's the good news. Your anxieties about birth and your ever-growing belly may ironically cause you to have sexy and erotic dreams. According to *The Mother-to-Be Dream Book*, by Raina Paris, experts say that these dreams are your subconscious attempts to reassure yourself that despite your itchy, bitchy hugeness, you're still sexy. So don't feel self-conscious about these dreams—enjoy them while you have them!

THE WHOLE TRUTH AND NOTHING BUT
Leakage as foreplay?

Before there may have been a few drips, but by now, some women have very leaky breasts, and this may be another sexual complication for you. You might feel like the last thing you want is nipple stimulation. Your S.O. may feel awkward too—feeling like, "That's my child's milk." Or, he may be very turned on at your wet nipples. Some couples do enjoy a boost in their sex life because of it. Both responses—the ick and ahh—are normal, even if no one talks about the ahh.

AT THIS POINT
Your back hurts (a lot!)

Here's another impediment to sex in the third trimester—your aching back. You may want to invest in some serious maternity support underwear or a maternity belt designed to give you some much-needed third trimester belly and back support. The underwear looks like an old-fashioned girdle, but if it helps your back, so what? (Who knows? Maybe all the straps will be a turn on for your S.O.)

Maternity belts are designed to sit right under your belly and are adjustable (read: expandable). You can find them where most maternity underwear is sold.

And if the idea of a maternity "girdle" makes you squeamish, remember: Up until the early 1900s, pregnant women wore corsets. Now *that* would be uncomfortable.

ADVICE FROM THE TRENCHES
More evidence that you can't win

> *"I've been pregnant twice and each time carried small. People were constantly commenting on my small size. They would say, 'Is the baby okay?' or 'You should eat more,' as if I was on a diet! Mostly, I just plastered a smile on my face and said, 'Thanks for your concern, but we're fine.'"*
> —Christine, mom to Julie and Maddie

AT THIS POINT
Your coworkers may be treating you like a side show

One of the most frustrating aspects of working late into your third trimester (besides the discomfort and distraction) may be your coworkers. The bigger you get, the more they will drive you crazy with comments. For them, your pregnancy, as well as your growing size, is a novelty and a distraction. Try to keep in mind that they probably mean no harm. But if their comments are really getting to you, just say something like, "I know you don't mean any harm, but I am just really tired of the comments, okay?"

TO-DO LIST
Send a passive-aggressive group e-mail

If the direct approach ("Shut up!") doesn't work at work, consider sending a passive-aggressive e-mail to all of your coworkers stating: "Unless you want to experience the joy of my 'water' breaking on the floor of your cubicle, I suggest you refrain from any further comments about my size, shape, or eating habits. Thank you for your attention to this matter."

That should take care of it!

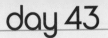

ADVICE FROM THE TRENCHES
Create a work-at-home opportunity

"I worked in the records department of a hospital before my kids were born. I was able to get medical transcription work for home at night after my kids were born because I knew some doctors. If you type well, you can often get work at home. Doctors and lawyers always need extra help."
—Tracy, mom to Jake, Paul, and Shannon

HOW TO BE REALISTIC ABOUT YOUR MATERNITY LEAVE

There's a reason why experienced moms snicker at pregnant women when it comes to things like working at home. Mostly, it's because moms know how much time newborn babies suck up, even though all they do is eat, poop, and sleep. No matter how much you tell yourself, "I'll be more organized," you're bound to wind up in your bathrobe at three in the afternoon, with laundry everywhere and a crying baby. Try not to make any regular work commitments about checking your e-mail daily or doing conference calls. You really are going to need and want your time with your baby.

TO-DO LIST
Start thinking of baby product inventions

If you're wishing that you never have to see your coworkers again after all of this, then become an inventor. Once your baby is on a schedule (around four to six months), start inventing the product that you wish you could have had during pregnancy. For inspiration and some fun products, check out the www.inventiveparent.com Web site. These are parents who took their ideas to market and made a mint. If they can do it, why not you?

day 42

AT THIS POINT

What is your baby doing?

As of 34 weeks, your baby weighs about 5 pounds (2.2 kg) and is probably about 19 1/2 inches (49 cm) long.

Lanugo, the ultra-fine hair that covers your baby's body, is starting to decrease—but the vernix caseosa, that slippery cheesy coating, is getting thicker in preparation for delivery.

Also by now, your baby is dreaming quite a bit. Researchers have discovered that babies are probably dreaming as early as week 25, when rapid eye movement sleep is first observed. Babies may also make faces in response to their dreams. Naturally, moms-to-be wonder, "Can my baby dream about me?" (Though there's no scientific evidence, all moms-to-be like to think the answer is yes.)

HOW TO SEE YOUR BABY'S FACE

Take a nap and dream! Many women will dream about their babies in the third trimester. Studies show that women see their babies in about 15 percent of their dreams. You may even have a dream that accurately depicts aspects of your future labor and delivery. How accurate are you? That's hard to tell, but some women do swear that they have accurate dreams of what their babies end up looking like. If you dream that your baby looks like Winston Churchill, don't panic—most newborns kind of look like Winston Churchill. Anxiety-induced nightmares are also common in the third trimester. These spooky dreams don't contain prophetic material. So the rule of thumb is: If the dream makes you happy, enjoy the feeling. If your dream is unpleasant, chalk it up to nervousness.

DOCTOR'S ORDERS
Learn the basics about epidurals

"You may be thinking about—or definitely planning on—having an epidural. The epidural is a small catheter or tube that is threaded through a needle into the space surrounding the spinal cord. It is not actually in the spinal cord fluid. These days most women receive an initial bolus or dose to gain pain control and then a continuous infusion that provides relief until after delivery. Many hospitals offer 'walking' epidurals now, which block the sensation of pain but not control of the actual muscles. This means you can possibly walk around, or at the very least have control of your legs, so you can push more effectively. As you can imagine, pushing while numb can be quite strange!"
—K.N.

THE WHOLE TRUTH AND NOTHING BUT
Epidurals may hurt

It will happen behind you, so you won't be able to see what's going on. (A good thing because the needle is big!) You will get a local shot before the big needle goes in, although some women do report still having a lot of pain from the procedure itself. Unfortunately, you don't really know how it's going to go for you until you're in the situation. But everyone agrees—epidural pain is a lot better than labor pain.

day 40

THE WHOLE TRUTH AND NOTHING BUT
The downside of epidurals

Three bummers about epidurals:

1. You might not be able to get one the second you ask—or scream—for one. First you need an IV placed so the nurse can give you intravenous fluids so your blood pressure won't drop. By then, hopefully, the anesthesiologist is available and ready. But the time between requesting an epidural and actually receiving one can be thirty or forty minutes, sometimes even longer. It can seem like an eternity when you're in pain.

2. To receive an epidural, you must either lie curled in a ball or sit on the edge of your bed leaning over with a pillow pressed into your belly. Either way, you need to be perfectly still. This is no problem if you're not having a contraction. But chances are, you will experience a whopper at some time during this procedure. Although many people describe this as "uncomfortable," a more accurate description is "*Hell.*" However, once the anesthesia is up and running in your system—which may happen right away or take another twenty or thirty minutes—it's sunshine and happiness for your next contraction. You'll look at the monitor and laugh!

3. While the doctor inserts the needle, which can take anywhere from five to ten minutes on average, your S.O. is often sent out of the room. Great! There you are, trying not to move, in the worst position possible, in pain, and there's no one to hold your hand. That's hard.

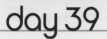

DOCTOR'S ORDERS
Know that epidurals have side effects

"One thing that many women are not prepared for is that epidurals can have side effects. You can vomit, get a bad headache, or even have a drop in blood pressure. Sometimes the baby doesn't like it, and he drops his heart rate. This is temporary and is usually corrected with increased intravenous fluids, position change, and some supplemental oxygen through the nose.

"But the most uncomfortable side effect happens when your epidural wears off. Many women get the shakes or intense shivering or itching, and they're not ready for it. You may experience freezing cold, and the nurses will pile blankets on you. It's not the end of the world, and it usually lasts for less than an hour, but it's nice to know it can happen so that when it starts, you don't panic and think you're having a seizure."
—K.N.

ADVICE FROM THE TRENCHES
Take it!

"Take the epidural. Or at least keep an open mind. I know some women are against it, but since I really didn't know what to expect, I didn't take it as soon as it was offered . . . and I was quite ready for it by the time I asked for it!"
—Michelle, mom to Emily

ADVICE FROM THE TRENCHES

What surprised me . . .

"My epidural wore off one hour before I delivered. The anesthesiologist was not available to come and give me more. That was a bad surprise. That last hour really hurt."
—Chrissy, mom to Caroline, Conner, and Cailey

"My first epidural didn't take. After I got the second one, I was so numb I couldn't even move my behind. When it was time to push, the doctor kept saying, 'Okay, just skooch down here closer to the end of the table.' I was thinking, 'What medical school did you go to?' I just kept saying, 'I can't feel my behind!' Because I had two epidurals, I was numb for about eight hours after delivery, and that was not fun."
—Corinne, mom to Katelyn, Emily, and Lauren

"Another fun thing: If you have an epidural, you can't tell when you have gas. The nurses actually come in and push on your stomach to try and get the gas out."
—Natalie, mom to Brent, Hayden, and Laney

"All that shaking when it wore off. That was scary."
—Dawn, mom to Sophia and Ava

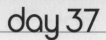

HOW TO FIND A PEDIATRICIAN

You need to have your baby's doctor lined up before you give birth, because you will need to take him for his first visit within a few days of leaving the hospital. Often your best resource for finding a pediatrician is other moms. Your doctor, midwife, and even your hospital's Web site are other good resources.

Remember, your baby's doctor has to take care of your needs, too. You want a doctor who will offer you reassurance and support.

TO-DO LIST

Buy at least one good medical parenting book

Check out books from accredited sources detailing first aid information, symptoms, development, and other important health care information for babies. You will pretty much have this book open every day, possibly several times a day, for the first few months of your baby's life.

ADVICE FROM THE TRENCHES

Pediatric nurses are so important

"Whatever you do, at least for your baby's first year, choose a practice with a nurse or nurse practitioner who is always available by phone. You quickly realize that you would call your pediatrician ten times a day if your husband would let you. Getting a nurse on the phone is so helpful. She can tell you what to do and if you need to come in without waiting for a doctor to call you back (which can take forever)."
—Karen, mom to Jenna

THE WHOLE TRUTH AND NOTHING BUT
Is it true that new fathers are jealous?

It's not a myth that many new dads feel shut out. It may sound ridiculous, but this jealousy can cause a lot of tension. Ideally you would like your partner to grow up and get with the program, but wishful thinking doesn't make it so. The truth is you both need each other as a couple away from the baby. Try to keep the lines of communication open. Plan ahead for when you are feeling better to spend time alone. Even though you won't be interested in sex for a while after birth, try to maintain some close physical intimacy. You and your partner will reap huge benefits by reaching out to each other.

HOW TO INSPIRE YOUR S.O.

If your S.O. is having jitters about being in the labor room, tell him this story: For centuries, men not only were not allowed in the labor room, they were legally barred from entering. But one intrepid doctor—Dr. Wertt of Hamburg in 1522— was so anxious to be in the labor room that he dressed as a woman and snuck in. He was caught and burned at the stake.

That story ought to provide your S.O. with some much-needed perspective!

AT THIS POINT
Need some bonding?

Ask your partner to paint your toenails. Not only will this cheer you up and give you some intimacy, it may be the only time in your entire relationship when he'll willingly do this.

day 35

AT THIS POINT
What's happening with your baby?

As you begin your 35th week of pregnancy, your baby weighs about 5½ pounds (2.5 kg) and measures 20 inches (nearly 51 cm) from head to toe. While she probably won't get too much longer, she still has some weight to put on, about a half a pound (.2 kg) per week until she makes her big debut.

THE WHOLE TRUTH AND NOTHING BUT
Your feet are the same size as your baby

At least they feel that big and long by now.

According to many podiatrists, swollen feet (edema) and flat feet are the two biggest pregnancy-related feet issues. The cause? Hmm . . . let's see . . . could it be *your weight* flattening your feet and *your giant uterus* changing your circulatory system so that fluid is retained in your feet?

HOW TO TREAT YOUR FEET

To relieve your swollen feet, wear wide shoes, keep your feet elevated whenever you're sitting or lying down, walk regularly for exercise, avoid salt and fats, and drink lots of water. For flat feet, get some good supportive athletic shoes or ready-made orthotics (inserts for your shoes that support and cushion).

day 34

AT THIS POINT
You're wondering if breastfeeding is for you

Today, many people—health professionals and nonprofessionals alike—have quite strong opinions about breastfeeding and why you should do it. It's easy to feel guilty, inadequate, selfish, or like a failure if you choose to bottle feed, or end up trying to breastfeed your baby and giving it up.

The truth is, both breastfeeding and bottle feeding are responsible choices. Regardless of what anyone tells you, breastfeeding has advantages *and* disadvantages. Here they are, in a nutshell:

Advantages: It's natural. Many women find it to be a beautiful bonding experience. It's healthy for your baby. Your colostrum has antibodies and immune boosters for your baby. Research has shown that breastfed babies get fewer ear infections and have fewer allergies and other health issues. Breastfeeding can aid in natural weight loss for mom. You don't have to deal with bottles or warm up formula in the middle of the night. Last but not least, it's free.

Disadvantages: You're the only one who can feed your baby (unless you express your milk), so all of the nighttime feedings are on you. You don't get your body back until you stop. You may need to eat even more than in pregnancy. You can't drink alcohol or take certain medications. Breastfeeding is a big commitment and can be very difficult in the beginning.

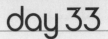

AT THIS POINT
Consider a nursing bra

Even if you're unsure whether or not you want to breastfeed, a nursing bra, with openings on the cups themselves to provide the baby nipple access, provides great support for your breasts when your milk comes in and you really swell up.

DOCTOR'S ORDERS
Make the decision that's best for you

"My patients always ask me, 'Is breastfeeding really better for my baby's health? What's in colostrum? Why is it healthy?' If you think about it, your breast milk is made exactly for your baby and adjusts as your baby grows. This is pretty incredible when everything goes well. The best advice I can give is to educate yourself as much as possible about breastfeeding before you get to your due date. Go to a breastfeeding class and bring your partner. The more information your partner has, the more support you will have. Nurses and doctors don't always give the best breastfeeding advice, so if there are any questions, ask for more help or ask to see a lactation consultant. Since your hospital stay is short, you have a very limited time to master the basics. But whatever you decide, you should feel comfortable with your decision and not feel pressured."
—K.N.

ADVICE FROM THE TRENCHES
Beware of surprise showers!

"I didn't realize my nipple would work like a shower head; I thought I would grow a special opening or something."
—Meg, mom to Christopher, Patrick, and Erin

ADVICE FROM THE TRENCHE*S*
Breastfeeding for me

"If I didn't have my sister to reassure me that it would get better in a few weeks, I would have quit. I'm so glad I didn't, because once you and the baby get the hang of it, it's wonderful. My lactation consultant wasn't really honest about what to expect. I think she was afraid that if you know it's hard and it hurts, you won't try it."
—Jessica, mom to Tyler

"For me, nothing about breastfeeding came naturally, and I am not a terribly patient person. I ended up giving it up after a week of trying and then went to formula. My children are no worse for the wear, and I am thankful I had this option. If it works for you, great. If not, don't beat yourself up."
—Marianne, mom to Patrick and Andy

"Besides the health benefits, one reason I chose to breastfeed was to save money. Formula is expensive!"
—Diane, mom to Robin and Ebon

"I am just one of these women who does not enjoy nipple stimulation of any kind. For me, it's almost painful. Breastfeeding wasn't even an option for me."
—Anonymous mom

"I was surprised by how long it takes the baby to catch on. I mean, they're the ones with the incentive! It took a good month before my daughter and I got the hang of it."
—Raveena, mom to Malika

"My son latched on right away, but he was a big eater. I had to feed him all the time. Pumping was also difficult and time consuming. Though I had planned on breastfeeding for six months, I gave it up after four. I was relieved, but I also felt guilty. Now that he's two, I see that he's fine and that I had no reason to feel badly."
—Gina, mom to Luca

day 31

TO-DO LIST
Buy a few kinds of baby bottles

There are so many kinds of baby bottles available. Some claim to reduce gas, but since all babies burp and spit up a lot, it's hard to tell if that's true. In the beginning you may want to have three different kinds of bottles on hand to discover the brand and style that your baby likes best.

ADVICE FROM THE TRENCHES
People will ask!

"Be prepared for everyone, even total strangers, to ask you if you're breastfeeding. When I would say, 'No,' they would often lecture me! It used to give me great pleasure to tell them that my son, who is now three, has never had an ear infection, and he's also developed a close bond with me and his father (who provided many of the bottle feedings)."
—Renee, mom to Glen

THE WHOLE TRUTH AND NOTHING BUT
You'll know when your milk comes in!

The expression "when your milk comes in" makes you think that there's a milkman making a friendly delivery on a scheduled day. In reality, there is no set time when breast milk will replace colostrum, though it usually occurs within three to five days of birth.

You'll know your milk has arrived because one day you'll wake up and you'll have hot torpedoes under your shirt. This is called *engorgement*. Engorgement is temporary but not fun. It's painful and can even cause fever or flu-like symptoms for a day.

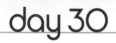# day 30

AT THIS POINT
You're wondering how breastfeeding affects your breasts

Breastfeeding often gets blamed for sagging breasts, but nursing does not affect the size of your breasts. Some studies, in fact, have shown that breastfeeding and gradual weaning make it more likely that fat will be redeposited in your breasts, helping them to regain more of their pre-pregnancy appearance. But as you know oh so well by now, breastfeeding is no guarantee that your breasts won't sag, because in pregnancy *there are no guarantees*.

As for your nipples, they will go back to their usual size and will probably lose some of the pigmentation they gained during pregnancy.

THE WHOLE TRUTH AND NOTHING BUT
You *will* have some sagging

Genetics, skin elasticity, and weight gain all influence how you'll look later. But truthfully, even if you're relatively small-breasted, and even if you breastfeed from day one, you will lose some of the elasticity in your breasts. Some degree of sagging is inevitable for every postpartum mom. Try to think of it as a small price to pay for having this beautiful little person in your life. (If that doesn't help, there's always a breast-lift operation later on.)

ADVICE FROM THE TRENCHES
Talk about sagging!

"After I had my breasts lifted, it slimmed my waistline too. Suddenly, I didn't have to tuck my breasts into my pants anymore."
—Patricia Heaton, actress and mom of four boys

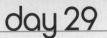

THE WHOLE TRUTH AND NOTHING BUT
Rocking chairs still work

Many pregnant women start to believe that unless they have the expensive glider with matching ottoman, they won't be able to breastfeed. (Remember the vortex, ladies!) Then there you are four months later whipping out your breast in the ladies' room of a restaurant while sitting on the commode because there's no chair. So if you can't spring for a pricey glider, don't worry about it. A good old-fashioned rocking chair gotten on the cheap from a thrift store works well too.

TO-DO LIST
Buy the biggest tube of Lansinoh you can find

If you know that you want to breastfeed, you should go to the hospital with the biggest tube of Lansinoh Breastfeeding Ointment you can buy. Start using it right away, after each time you nurse. You don't have to wipe it off for your baby's next feeding, and some women swear it made all the difference in being able to stick with breastfeeding through the first painful weeks.

ADVICE FROM THE TRENCHES
Buy some formula, just in case

"I knew I wanted to breastfeed my first baby—and I did for a year—but I also didn't know what to expect. When I left the hospital, I asked the nurse for some of the little disposable bottles with formula in them. I figured I didn't want to be at home and not have the options or the means to feed my baby if the breastfeeding didn't work."
—Wendy, mom to Shyanne

day 28

AT THIS POINT
You're 36 weeks pregnant!

By now, most babies weigh around 6 pounds (around 2.7 kg) and are 20 1/2 inches (52 cm) long.

With one month to go, all of his senses are well-developed. He has a sense of taste. All of his body parts are sensitive to hot and cold and pressure. When he's born, he'll be able to see your face when it's 6 inches (15 cm) from his, although your specific features will be still be tough for him to see. He's been hearing a wide range of sounds for the last several weeks.

While your baby puts the finishing touches on his development, your body is getting ready for labor. Starting this week, your doctor or midwife will check your cervix for effacement (or thinning) and dilation (opening)—signs that you may be going into labor soon.

THE WHOLE TRUTH AND NOTHING BUT
You may not want a C-section!

Though elective ("sign me up!") C-sections are on the rise—some women want the convenience of scheduling and also want to avoid pelvic floor issues like incontinence—many women have very strong feelings about not having a C-section. Which is understandable—after all, it's surgery, which has potential complications and risks.

But what if you don't dilate on your own? Or what if you do, but your baby is breech (that is, positioned feet-first in the birth canal?) As your countdown day gets closer, you may be intent on avoiding a surgical birth. C-sections have become controversial. Advocates of natural birth say that this surgery is unnecessary, and in some cases, maybe it is. But what you need to know is that if you stop dilating despite pitocin, your baby doesn't descend, or there is any kind of fetal distress or placental problem, you will need to have a C-section, and it could save you and your baby from serious complications.

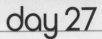

ADVICE FROM THE TRENCHES
My one regret

"I found out my son was breech and that I needed a C-section. I don't regret having given birth this way, and in fact, my recovery was fast. What I regret was not being prepared for it. It would have been so much less scary if I had known what to expect."
—Jen, mom to Jack and Madison

THE WHOLE TRUTH AND NOTHING BUT
Do they really tie your arms down?

This is something that scares women to death—and with good reason! What really happens is that your arms will be tied (with gauze, not rope) out to the side, so your nurses can have access to your IV (this is especially common if you're getting the shakes from your epidural). While you may feel like you are being tortured, most of the time your arms don't need to be tied down. And if you tell your doctor and nurse you don't want to be tied down, they'll usually honor that request.

HOW TO FOCUS ON THE POSITIVE

After a C-section, you may feel that you did something wrong during your pregnancy that led you to a surgical delivery. This is simply not the case. Some C-sections are unavoidable no matter how healthy you are, how well you ate, or how much you exercised.

On the positive side, you won't experience any of the weakening of the pelvic floor, which can cause incontinence, among other things. You won't be stretched out and grabbing your crotch when you sneeze.

HOW TO MENTALLY PREPARE YOURSELF—JUST IN CASE!

Labor is no time for a crash course in C-sections. Here are the basics of how you will be prepped:

* Once you get the word, things will happen very fast. Ten nurses will seem to come out of the woodwork. They'll wheel you into a freezing cold operating room. They'll insert an IV in your arm or hand and a catheter into your bladder to empty it. You'll be handed a consent form to sign.

* If you hadn't already received an epidural, and you're not in an emergency, an anesthesiologist will come in and will administer one, so you can be numb from the waist down but mentally alert. However, though it's less common, if there's any question about your baby's immediate health, things will need to move very quickly; in that case, you may be given a general anesthetic, which will put you "under."

* Now you'll be laying there pretty much naked for the entire world, under very bright lights. (Remember, the ten-plus people in the room with you really have seen it all.) Your abdomen will be cleaned with an antiseptic solution. You may get shaved beforehand, and no, not your legs, ladies (it's the growing back part that you'll notice more, anyway). There will be some drapes that separate your upper body from your lower half to ensure that the incision stays sterile.

* If your C-section was planned in advance—or if it was unplanned, but not an emergency—most doctors and hospitals will allow your partner to stay with you. Your S.O. will be asked to put on a special suit and can sit beside you during the procedure. You will probably have an oxygen mask on, which will make it hard to speak, but at least your S.O. can be there to comfort you.

DOCTOR'S ORDERS
Behind the scenes at your C-section

"Your doctor will make a small horizontal incision in your skin above your pubic bone (called a bikini cut). Then, she will cut through the various layers of your abdominal wall to get to your uterus. You will feel pressure and tugging sensations, but you should not feel pain. If you do feel pain, tell your anesthesiologist or nurse anesthetist, who will be sitting right by you so they can administer more medicine through your epidural or IV.

"Then, it's time for your baby to make his grand entrance! While it should seem fairly easy to deliver the baby, you will be amazed by the amount of tugging and pulling you may feel. Babies are slippery and have a way of wedging themselves into certain positions. Sometimes, believe it or not, doctors have to use a vacuum or forceps to deliver the baby.

"While the staff is examining your baby, your doctor delivers the placenta and then starts sewing everything back together. All the sutures inside your abdomen will dissolve over time. Your skin incision will either have absorbable sutures, staples, or special glue.

"If there are no complications, the entire procedure takes about thirty or forty minutes. From the time your incision is made until your baby is delivered usually takes less than ten minutes. You can expect to remain in the hospital for four days.

"Don't be scared if you don't feel very emotional about your baby right away, I promise you, with time that will change."

—K.N.

day 24

AT THIS POINT
How is your baby evaluated?

After a C-section, the nurses will dry him and warm him under light warmers so that his body temperature regulates itself. They will suction his nose and mouth to remove the extra fluid and will make sure he is breathing well. His umbilical cord will be clamped closer to his navel and your partner will have the opportunity to cut it.

No matter how you deliver, by C-section or vaginally, your baby's appearance and health will be checked immediately in five areas (known as the APGAR test): heart rate, breathing, muscle tone, reflexes, and skin color.

THE WHOLE TRUTH AND NOTHING BUT
When will you get to hold your baby?

After your baby is delivered, it can take what seems like a lifetime—about one hour—before you get to hold him. After you're stitched up, you'll be wheeled into a recovery room, where you can finally hold your baby either on your chest or in your arm like a football. Unfortunately, you may get the epidural shakes and not be able to focus on your baby when you first have the chance.

If there were issues about your baby's health that led to a C-section, your baby will be checked out and possibly spend some time in the NICU, so you may not get to hold him for several hours (which may feel like an eternity). But you have to remind yourself that he's getting the best care possible, and you'll be together very soon.

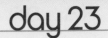

AT THIS POINT
You're wondering if they will slap her behind

Only in old movies. During both a C-section and vaginal birth the mouth and nose are suctioned so she can breathe easier and "pink up."

DOCTOR'S ORDERS
Give yourself time to bond

"I thought the reason I didn't bond immediately with my daughter was because I had a C-section. It was at least forty-eight hours later before I felt that intense maternal love. Later, when I was taking care of a laboring woman, her mother and two aunts started talking about how no one talks about delayed bonding. I was surprised to learn that they had had vaginal deliveries! These women taught me what I didn't learn in med school. I was normal, and my cesarean had nothing to do with it. Bonding is not always instant!"
—K.N.

THE WHOLE TRUTH AND NOTHING BUT
C-section recovery is painful

After a C-section, you'll be in pain and very sore for a few days, and you'll need painkillers. The first morning after your C-section, a nurse will take out your urinary catheter (no pain). Then she'll make you sit up, get up, and walk (lots of pain). Many women will tell you that the first time out of bed is the worst, but after the first forty-eight hours, progress is rapid. Many are able to get up and shower the day after the surgery. The more you move around, the better you will feel.

DOCTOR'S ORDERS
Most S.O.s do great

"So many dads are amazed that they can actually watch the surgery, they just can't help themselves. They are mesmerized by the delivery. Also let your S.O. know that he will be a source of grounding and strength for you.

"Understandably, watching you have surgery may be too difficult for some people to handle. But reassure your S.O. that it's fine for him to focus on you until the baby is delivered. Warn your partner that he may see a lot of blood and your baby may look very blue when he is first delivered. Don't worry, almost every baby delivered by cesarean looks this way. Once he starts crying, either immediately or when he is with the nurses, he will 'pink up.'"
—K.N.

ADVICE FROM THE TRENCHES
On the subject of C-sections . . .

"I was surprised to discover that you have to ask for painkillers; they don't just come in every six hours and hand them over. You definitely want to stay on top of that."
—Jen, mom to Jack and Madison

"Make sure you know about the hospital's policy on what happens if you have a C-section and can't nurse your baby right away. I had one, and wasn't allowed to feed my daughter while in the recovery room. Next time, I'll know to specify."
—Anonymous mom

"Your pain medicine causes constipation, so take the stool softeners when offered. It hurts to push after a C-section."
—Natalie, mom to Brent, Hayden, and Elena

day 21

AT THIS POINT
She's almost ready, and so are you!

At week 37, your baby weighs about 6 1/2 pounds (2.9 kg). She's now considered full term. Full term means your baby is fully developed and could be born at any time. (Though remember, most first-time moms are late.) You should be done with your childbirth education class by now. Make sure you get that pediatrician lined up. You'll need to take the baby for her first appointment within a few days of being released from the hospital.

TO-DO LIST
Learn another pregnancy misnomer: *lightening*

There is nothing "light" about the feeling of a baby dropping into your pelvis. Some women describe the feeling as, "Suddenly I feel like there's a watermelon in my behind."

Actually, the lightening you're hoping for—because it means the baby is getting ready to drop into the birth canal—is when the baby starts to settle deeper into your pelvis. This new position lowers your center of gravity and relieves some of the pressure on your diaphragm; it's called *lightening* because you may actually feel lighter—up high anyway—and like you can breathe more easily again.

THE WHOLE TRUTH AND NOTHING BUT
You didn't think it was possible, but . . .

. . . you actually have to pee even more now! As your baby settles down into your pelvis you may have an easier time breathing, but she's pressing harder on your bladder.

day 20

DOCTOR'S ORDERS
Don't worry if your baby hasn't dropped by now

"Lightening may occur weeks before the onset of labor, or any time right up until the day labor begins. It may be noticeable enough that others comment on your changed appearance, or you might not be aware of it at all."
—K.N.

AT THIS POINT
You're wondering what labor is really like

There's a reason why it's called *labor* and not *vacation*. It's important to understand that for every woman, labor is a unique experience. The one common denominator, however, is that childbirth is usually painful. You'll learn this in childbirth class. What they sometimes don't tell you is that childbirth is also the bloodiest, messiest, and sweatiest event of your entire life. All sorts of fluids and solids, matter, and goo will emerge from your body. But don't worry—so will your baby, eventually.

THE WHOLE TRUTH AND NOTHING BUT
What do contractions feel like?

Ask one hundred women to describe contractions, and you'll get one hundred different answers, but here are a few of the most common descriptions: like period cramps but to the tenth power, extreme gas pains, intense pressure, burning, or a combination of all of these sensations.

HOW TO PREPARE YOURSELF FOR PUSHING

If you don't have an epidural numbing you, you will feel the urge to push or bear down. The pushing stage of your labor happens after the cervix is completely dilated (open) and no longer in front of your baby's head. If you are numb, you won't have the sensation to push, but your labor nurse or doctor will tell you when to push.

Midwives often refer to the sensation of pushing your baby out as the *ring of fire*. Many women say that they thought that pushing would bring relief, but it didn't; they felt an intense burning sensation instead. You may also feel like you're going to have a major BM right then and there, and many women do. Some women say they felt like they were going to pop a blood vessel from pushing. It's hard work getting a baby to the outside world.

THE WHOLE TRUTH AND NOTHING BUT

Poop happens!

It's very common to have a BM or to urinate while having a contraction or pushing. Lovely! Here is what every woman who has pooped before you has learned: Your doctor and labor nurses have seen it all. They are not fazed by your bodily functions and can clean them up almost as quickly as they come out. Most likely if you do have a BM, you won't really care and may not even notice. You will have other things on your mind. Let this be the least of your worries.

day 18

THE WHOLE TRUTH AND NOTHING BUT
How long does labor last?

The big question! For first-time moms, the first stage of labor—from the start of contractions to your cervix being fully open and ready—takes on average anywhere from *ten to fourteen* hours. But remember, some of this stage will happen at home. (After you are sent back there, in tears, by your doctor or midwife, because you're not far enough along.)

The second stage of labor is your pushing stage and usually takes about one to two hours; it just feels like ten.

The third stage begins when your baby is delivered and lasts until the placenta is delivered, and on average, it takes about fifteen to thirty minutes, though sometimes longer.

Some women get to have their babies placed on their bellies immediately upon delivery; others minutes after the baby is dried and wrapped in a blanket like a burrito.

DOCTOR'S ORDERS
Ask your S.O. if he wants to cut the cord

"Having your S.O. cut the cord once your baby is born is a wonderful way to make him feel directly involved in his baby's birth. He may understandably be a little fearful or squeamish, so let him know that there are no nerve endings in the umbilical cord. Neither you or the baby will feel a thing. Many moms and partners are worried that if the cord isn't cut properly that their baby will end up with an 'outie.' How the cord is cut has no bearing on the appearance of the bellybutton. The other positive—he'll have professional guidance and help."
—K.N.

HOW TO DELIVER THE PLACENTA

It doesn't just stay in there!

After your baby is born and the cord is cut, you'll still have contractions, though not nearly as painful. A lot of women completely forget, or have little memory of, this part of labor. At that point all of your attention is, naturally, focused on your baby, whom you will probably be holding.

Your placenta separates from the wall of your uterus. You may feel an urge to push or your doctor or midwife may tell you to push, massage your stomach, or if all else fails, reach in and take it out.

In case you're wondering, the placenta looks like a big piece of raw meat with a shiny membrane around it. You can ask to see it if you're curious.

DOCTOR'S ORDERS
Be prepared for tearing or an episiotomy

"Episiotomies used to be performed routinely because it was always thought that a clean cut was better than many irregular tears. Most of us are finally realizing that if you allow the perineum to stretch slowly as the head crowns or delivers you will avoid a significant tear even with a first baby. Cutting an episiotomy actually can make you more susceptible to a worse tear. There are certain situations where an episiotomy is necessary, such as with fetal distress, a large baby, or with a forceps delivery. Don't worry if your doctor feels an episiotomy is necessary; she will administer a local anesthetic if you don't have an epidural."
—K.N.

day 16

ADVICE FROM THE TRENCHES
The labor after labor

"It's the part no one talks about . . . about how hard it is to recover from a vaginal birth and how much it hurts. For my first and third, it took several weeks for the pain to go away."
—Corinne, mom to Katelyn, Emily, and Lauren

THE WHOLE TRUTH AND NOTHING BUT
Your traumatized vagina

If you deliver vaginally, your vagina is going to be traumatized. It's not permanent, but for a few weeks at least, it's going to hold a grudge!

You think about labor and what it will be like to bring a baby home—but not what your own recovery will be like. When you discover how painful it is, it can be overwhelming—especially because it's hard to take care of your exhausted self with a new baby in the house.

HOW TO DEAL WITH YOUR STITCHES

Your vaginal stitches will usually dissolve in about five days. (Could you imagine if they had to be removed?) In the hospital, you'll most likely be put on the standard pads–ice pack regime. Witch hazel pads, sold under the brand name Tucks, are soothing, and the ice packs reduce the swelling. When you get home, you need to do warm "sitz" baths, where you sit in the tub with water covering just your buttocks and hips. These mini baths are important for two reasons: First, they help with pain and prevent infection. But more importantly, they force you to sit still and not do anything else! Wiping yourself with toilet paper will be an agony, so you'll need a spray bottle filled with water. You will also need a cushion for sitting.

day 15

TO-DO LIST
Pregnancy term of the day: lochia

You pronounce it *LOW-key-a* but there is nothing *low key* about it. Lochia—a mix of blood, mucus, and placenta leftovers—is the frightening bright red blood and clotty mess that spews forth from your body for about six weeks after your baby is born. After birth, the first time you walk from your bed to the bathroom, look behind you. Chances are you'll have left a pool of blood in your bed, on the floor, and all over the bathroom. Don't be scared. Don't be embarrassed. But above all, don't try to clean it up yourself. Call for help. (Your nurse is ready for this.)

DOCTOR'S ORDERS
Dealing with your bleeding at home

"The first few days after birth are especially heavy and messy. After that, you'll still need jumbo pads—but as long as you're not soaking a pad every one to two hours, you're normal. If you notice your bleeding increasing or you start passing large clots, this can be a sign that you are doing too much. Get off your feet and check your pads. If it doesn't slow down then, call your doctor. Very rarely, this can be a sign of retained placental fragments."
—K.N.

ADVICE FROM THE TRENCHES
The labor of lochia

"You'll get your pad on, your Tucks tucked in, and your ice pad in place—but as soon as you get back in bed, you'll have to pee again!"
—Allison, mom to Katie, Abby, Johnny, and one on the way

day 14

AT THIS POINT
You are 38 weeks pregnant!

What's happening now that you're in the home stretch? At your check-up this week, your doctor or midwife may report that your cervix has dilated a centimeter or two. But if it hasn't, don't despair. Your cervix will need to dilate ten centimeters before birth, but this process can happen slowly over time or within a few short hours.

Meanwhile, your baby is anywhere between 6 and 8 pounds (2.7–3.6 kg), and hopefully not too much more!

THE WHOLE TRUTH AND NOTHING BUT
Big babies do happen to small people

Just ask Francisca Ramos dos Santos. This thirty-eight-year-old Brazilian woman has one dubious distinction you won't envy. In January 2005, she gave birth to one of the world's largest newborns—16.7 pounds (7.6 kg)! That's around what a six-month-old weighs. Obviously (and mercifully), baby Ademilton was born by C-section. He and his average-sized mother are doing fine!

TO-DO LIST
Charge that cell phone!

In your last month of pregnancy, you and your S.O./birth partner should keep constant tabs on each other, just in case you go into labor sooner than expected. If your S.O. travels to an area where cell phone coverage is weak, consider investing in a pager.

THE WHOLE TRUTH AND NOTHING BUT
Your unpleasant recovery, continued . . .

By the end of this month, you may be convinced that Mother Nature is a man. Here are a few more of the symptoms you may experience after childbirth:

Bionic fatigue returns. The fatigue you experience after birth is intense. Think of what you've just been through physically, not to mention your heightened state of emotion.

Only boxers sweat more. If you find that you're waking up drenched, sleep with a pile of T-shirts and towels next to your bed.

There's a bunch of grapes in your behind. Hemorrhoids, caused by the strain of pushing.

You're peeing a monsoon. Your body needs to rid itself of all the extra fluid, and your bladder may have trouble emptying fully, because it became stretched out.

You don't always make it to the bathroom. After a vaginal birth, especially if you had a big baby, you won't have great control over your bladder or your BMs for a few weeks. Your pelvic floor was, well, floored by labor. This is embarrassing, gross, and often a bad surprise. But let your doctor know if it doesn't improve after six weeks.

Cramps (again). While your uterus returns to normal over the course of the next six weeks (at least something does!), you may feel contractions for a few weeks, especially if you're breastfeeding.

Hair loss. Sometimes it comes out in clumps, and you'll think you're going bald. You're not! It will stop when your hormones get back to normal.

day 12

TO-DO LIST
Line up some postpartum help—NOW!

It's great if your S.O. can take time off from work, but you're still going to need extra help for the first few weeks at least. You'll both be exhausted and overwhelmed.

If you can't afford to hire a doula, consider a cleaning service for a month to at least take care of your home. You can also hire a postpartum or mother's helper. They have references, and they do laundry and cook. Check your phone book for agencies.

When friends call and say, "Is there anything I can do?" tell the truth: "My house hasn't been vacuumed in two weeks" or "We need someone to grocery shop."

Hire a grandmother, a reliable neighbor, or a mom with school-aged kids to babysit or to help with the chores. Or just pay them so you can nap.

Your postpartum period may be the only time in your life when you'll be happy to have your mother or mother-in-law clean your house. Let her.

ADVICE FROM THE TRENCHES
It's okay to give up control

"Accept any help that is offered, because you will need it, even if you don't think you do or you (like me) like to be in control. You want to be able to enjoy the baby as much as you can—and at the beginning it's so difficult, with your own discomfort and sleep deprivation. Letting someone take care of some of the peripheral things really is a big help (even if you can't quite understand how your helper came up with the laundry-sorting system he did)."
—Michelle, mom to Emily

AT THIS POINT
You're worried you won't even know if you're in labor!

All this business about recovering from labor, and you're probably thinking, "But how will I even know when I'm *in* labor?"

Most moms will laugh and assure you, "Oh, you'll know!" And after you give birth, you will know. But for now, if this is your first child, you really don't know. And if your "water" doesn't break but you've been having strong Braxton Hicks contractions on and off for a few weeks, how are you supposed to guess?

The surprising truth is that for many women, it's really hard to know when you're in labor or when labor is starting if you've never been in labor before. Don't be embarrassed if you're on the phone with your doctor or midwife every day. That's why they're there, and you should always call.

THE WHOLE TRUTH AND NOTHING BUT
Your "water" probably won't break!

Though it happens a lot on TV, only one in twenty women will ever have their "water" break (a rupture of their amniotic sac). The other nineteen get assistance from the doctor or midwife.

DOCTOR'S ORDERS
When we do it for you . . .

"Having your membranes ruptured by your doctor can be very uncomfortable but not usually painful. The discomfort comes more from the actual vaginal exam."
—K.N.

ADVICE FROM THE TRENCHES
Sometimes you get lucky

"With my second child, I had cramps very low in my abdomen and also in my back. My doctor thought I might have a urinary tract infection. My husband and I took our time getting to the hospital. When we got there, we were shocked to discover that I was already ten centimeters dilated. Two hours later, I was holding my daughter."
—Shari, mom to Ryan and Rebecca

DOCTOR'S ORDERS
Recognizing the real thing

"The definition of true labor is regular painful contractions that cause cervical dilation. Generally, your doctor or midwife will be able to tell if you are in labor by examining your cervix over time to see if you have dilated. Often, it can be difficult to tell whether you are in true labor or having false labor. It's likely that you're having true labor if:

* *After timing the contractions, you determine that they are coming consistently, and getting closer together.*

* *Each contraction is lasting anywhere from thirty to seventy seconds and getting longer.*

* *Your contractions don't go away even if you change your level of activity.*

* *The contractions start in your lower back and radiate to the front.*

* *Your water breaks.*

"The intensity of the contractions becomes greater as time progresses. Usually, once you have been having painful contractions every five minutes for the past two to three hours, you can consider yourself in labor. This does not mean you are ready to deliver. You could still have many hours before you would be offered an epidural."
—K.N.

HOW TO TELL IF YOUR "WATER" BREAKS

Given the giant waves that seem to erupt from pregnant women on TV shows, you might think that your "water" breaking would be obvious. It probably won't surprise you to learn, given the unobvious nature of pregnancy, that many women aren't sure if it's happened or not.

You may feel a trickle of warm liquid. You could hear a "pop" and get a gush or a trickle. The problem is that the "squeeze when you sneeze" syndrome that you're also experiencing can make it hard to tell if your "water" broke or if your bladder did.

So put on a sanitary pad and lay down for twenty minutes. When you stand up, if you feel another trickle or gush, the chances are that your "water" did break.

If you're not sure, call your doctor. She really enjoys talking to you every day. Really!

TO-DO LIST
Learn to recognize your mucous plug

Another charming pregnancy term. The mucous plug fills the cervix to protect against disease and infection. This may start leaking out as the cervix slowly starts opening before labor, or may come out in one big chunk—lovely! It can be pink or tinged with blood. While it's not the most attractive thing to find on your underwear, it's a good sign!

day 8

TO-DO LIST
Time to pack

When to pack is one of those Pregnancy Land conundrums. Too early seems like a jinx, but you don't want to be running around like a maniac and doing laundry when you're in labor, either.

And what to pack? You're not going to Antarctica. However, once you're in the throes of labor, you won't be running to the gift shop for lollipops, either. Basically, bring anything and everything you think might make your labor and hospital stay more comfortable—mp3 player, magazines, a good luck charm.

Definitely leave your nice nightgown at home; it will only get ruined in the aftermath. Nice thick socks and slippers are a must. Hospital floors are frightening—partly because of all the blood you'll be leaving on them. But pack them knowing that you may be leaving them behind for the bio hazard guy to remove.

Don't forget your nursing bra and nursing pads—whether or not you're going to breastfeed, you'll need them when your milk comes in.

AT THIS POINT
Should you pack your own sanitary napkins?

Yes, unless your hospital supplies them for free as part of your overall hospital bill. Be warned: Hospital-issued pads look like miniature trampolines—and you're going to need them big. If you bring your own, super size them, bring a lot, and have a good supply at home, too.

AT THIS POINT
What's going on with your baby?

Absolutely nothing new! He's all plump and ready. Just snoozing and living off his mother. You, on the other hand, have now entered what some consider to be the most agonizing wait of your life.

THE WHOLE TRUTH AND NOTHING BUT
Mesh underwear awaits you!

If no one has told you about them, you'll be happy to know that you only have to pack a few pairs of your own underwear for wearing home because you'll be outfitted in disposable mesh underwear while in the hospital. This is the strangest looking underwear in the history of underwear. It's like wearing a hairnet. But once you start gushing blood, you'll understand the need for disposable.

Any of your own underwear that you pack should be your worst pairs, which you won't mind never seeing again. (Maternity underwear is a great choice!)

HOW TO BE A REALIST WHEN YOU JUST WANT TO BE THIN (OR AT LEAST NOT HUGE) AGAIN

Put your maternity jeans, shorts, or your favorite big pants in your suitcase. It's hard, but you need to do this. You can give life. You can manage labor. You're amazing! But you're not so amazing that you will be able to squeeze into your pre-preggo jeans unless you're going on a gurney from Labor and Delivery to the Plastic Surgery floor for liposuction and tummy tucking. If you don't need your maternity pants, that's fabulous. But if you need them and don't have them, you'll have to swing your belly over your arm to get out of the hospital!

ADVICE FROM THE TRENCHES

What to pack

"Food! Pack lots of snacks and large juice boxes. At meals they will give you these tiny cups of juice that don't come close to cutting your thirst."
—Vandette, mom to Jonathan

"Hospitals have the worst pillows! Buy an inexpensive but decent pillow just for taking to the hospital. Put an old or cheap pillowcase on it in case it gets lost."
—Gina, mom to Landis and Brandon

"Your own bathrobe! You will be so happy that you did. I had to wear a hospital gown backward as a robe until my husband brought mine."
—Karen, mom to Trevor and Sarah

"I'm so glad my sister warned me not to go home in a dress. You need the support of pants to hold your pad in place."
—Melissa, mom to Alyssa and Maya

"Both times, I forgot to pack an outfit for the baby to wear home! I had to talk my husband through picking out the outfits, and he got it all wrong."
—Margaret, mom to Shane and Colleen

"A girlfriend told me to bring my own favorite soap, shampoo, and conditioner because hospital toiletries stink. Hospital shampoo basically produces no lather. But I left my toothbrush at home because I didn't want to get it germy."
—Beth, mom to Scott

"For my second, I brought little picture frames, small gift books, and thank you cards to give to my nurses. You will absolutely fall in love with yours."
—Maris, mom to William and Lacey

"Some fresh clothes and a toothbrush for my husband."
—Laurie, mom to Anthony Jr.

AT THIS POINT
Start taking names for babysitters

Friends and family will say, "Once you two get settled, and if you want a night out, I'd love to babysit."

Don't just say, "Thanks!" Get your calendar or electronic organizer out and pick the date. Though when you first have your baby, you think, "I could never leave him with anyone else," around four months will go by and you will need a serious date night with your S.O.

HOW TO DECIDE ABOUT VISITORS

When you're in the hospital, your rule of thumb should be: Who will I not mind seeing me either (1) leaving a trail of blood on my way to the bathroom or (2) trying to get my baby to latch onto my swollen, leaky boob?

That leaves Uncle Pete out in the parking lot! You may want to keep the list of visitors strictly to very close relatives who are all warned about knocking and waiting to be told to come in.

TO-DO LIST
Create your Who to Call list

(This list will look suspiciously like your list of volunteer babysitters.)

Creating a list of people for your S.O. to call from the hospital is a great way to tell people about your good news—and an even better way to communicate that you're not ready for visitors. You can say, "We'll call you as soon as we get home." (Hint, hint!)

AT THIS POINT
It's time to install your infant car seat

Talk about nerves: When you're in the hospital, the last thing your S.O. will want to be doing is installing an infant car seat. This can take hours! It also takes two people—one to read the instructions, and one to follow them, one to doubt the proper installation, and one to reinstall it. (Save the instructions in case you have to move the seat to another car at some point!)

TO-DO LIST
Send your S.O. to the police station

Not to have him arrested, but to have him check out the car seat installation.

There is nothing more important than having your baby's car seat installed properly. Most communities have a police officer who is trained in proper car seat installation. If your community doesn't, contact your car dealer. Remember, you won't be allowed to leave the hospital with your baby unless you have a rear-facing infant car seat that's properly installed. (Your nurse will check.)

HOW TO CHEER YOURSELF UP

While your S.O. is dealing with the car seat, go to a real spa and get a pedicure. You will be amazed at the number of people who will, while you're in the hospital, comment on how cute your toes look. With the rest of you bloated and in a temporary state of discombobulation, pretty toes count.

HURRY UP AND WAIT ALERT
Will you or won't you?

Will you be late? Could this pregnancy possibly last any longer? The answer is yes—it probably will. This is truly the most agonizing wait in Pregnancy Land. You pretty much cry all the time and hate everyone.

AT THIS POINT
Your baby is packed, too

In a manner of speaking, that is. He's actually prepping for birth, too. When labor *finally* and mercifully starts, your baby will, unlike you, know exactly what to do.

First, his fetal hormones will rise so he'll be able to maintain his blood sugar and pressure levels. He will repress his practice breathing movements in order to store his energy for his big birthday entrance, and when the moment arrives, he will absorb the fluid in his lungs after his first breath. Pretty impressive.

THE WHOLE TRUTH AND NOTHING BUT
You should know . . .

If you have your baby in August or September, your chance of being sent home from the hospital in the early stages of labor are really high. The reason? These are the most popular months for giving birth, so the hospital or birthing center will be packed.

day 2

THE WHOLE TRUTH AND NOTHING BUT
Only Super Glue bonds instantly

Now that you are so close to the day when you will finally meet your baby, you need to remember that bonding with your baby—even if you have a vaginal delivery—often doesn't happen instantaneously. Bonding with your new baby can take several days, weeks, and even months.

Though "love at first sight" probably does happen for some women, remember that you're likely exhausted and experiencing side effects from your pain medication. You may not feel anything at all except relief that labor or your C-section is over. You may even be secretly thrilled that your S.O. is there to hold the baby, because you may not be able to focus on him until you're feeling a little more stable. It's okay; you'll bond later. The love is huge and needs to be absorbed and experienced over time. Otherwise, it would knock you off your feet.

ADVICE FROM THE TRENCHES
You may feel like you're in a bubble

"The minute Christopher was born, I vividly remember thinking, 'I can't believe there was really someone really in there! Now, he was over 9 pounds, and I was huge, so I don't know why I was so surprised. But actually seeing a baby hit me so hard—there really was a person in there. It's mind-blowing."
—Meg, mom to Christopher, Patrick, and Erin

AT THIS POINT
Your countdown day has arrived!

You've made it. For 280 days (more or less, anyway), you've survived all the ups and downs that Pregnancy Land has to offer. No matter what happens on this day, you've made a remarkable journey—and you're about to embark on another, even more amazing one—motherhood! All you want to do is meet your baby! And very soon you will.

TO-DO LIST
Take a minute to reflect

Take a deep breath and hold on to this moment. This moment could be the moment pregnancy ends and a whole new life begins. Soon you will have your labor story, a story that you will tell over and over again because you will have earned the right.

You are about to experience a rite of passage that bonds you with all other mothers. It will be the story you tell your child every year on the day that moment turned into the experience of a lifetime.

You will also learn that the fears don't end here but become endless once your baby is born. But that is all right, because that intense fear will also put you in complete awe every time you look into your baby's eyes.

You really are going to be a mother. And you really are going to be fantastic.

THE FOURTH TRIMESTER

1 day past due date

THE WHOLE TRUTH AND NOTHING BUT
Itchier, bitchier, and even bigger!

You have begun the "fourth trimester," the trimester you didn't know existed 281 days ago. (Sorry, someone has to break it to you: There is one more "trimester.") This is the surprise trimester no one talks about, the one that begins today and doesn't end until your baby shows up.

AT THIS POINT
Why you?

The likeliest reason is that your due date was miscalculated, and you're actually not even late, just right on schedule. Beyond that, it's still a mystery why some pregnant women seem to hang out longer than others. It's nothing you did wrong—blame it on Mother Nature. (Who you now know is a man impersonating a woman!)

ADVICE FROM THE TRENCHES
The end is finally knowable

"Though being overdue is agony second only to morning sickness, at least you know that you will have your baby, one way or another, within two weeks. The end is truly in sight."
—Clare, mom to Annie and Grace

2 days past due date

DOCTOR'S ORDERS
The onset of labor is still a mystery

"Being overdue is a frustrating time. You have made it through all the trimesters, and you really want to meet your baby. Naturally people always ask me, 'What starts labor?' I wish I could give a definitive answer. There are a number of factors that go into initiating labor, but no one knows the exact triggering event. It seems to come down to when the baby is ready, it sends a hormonal signal to mom and initiates a cascade of hormonal events that lead to labor.

"There are many signs that your body is getting ready, but none are indicative that labor will start soon after. You will hear your doctor talk a lot about cervical ripening—meaning it's becoming soft, thin, and dilated—when you are overdue.

"Many women ask why we don't just induce them as soon as they pass their due dates. The reason is, if you and your baby aren't ready for labor we can give all the pitocin (the synthetic form of oxytocin given through an IV) in the world, but it won't put you into labor. For induction to go smoothly, your doctor will want your cervix to be as ripe as possible. Until that happens, your doctor or midwife will want to wait and watch you closely."

—K.N.

THE WHOLE TRUTH AND NOTHING BUT

Does sex really bring baby?

Sex might be the thing that started it all, but can it finish it all?

With your size, level of discomfort, and *bad* mood, sex is not going to be a blast, so if you're going to do it (and can convince your partner to do it with you), you want to know if it will get labor rolling or not.

The answer is nobody knows, but given the sheer volume of women who will tell you they tried it and it didn't work, it probably doesn't work. Even despite the fact that sperm contains some prostaglandins, hormones that help in inducing labor, and having an orgasm releases oxytocin and stimulates a few contractions.

Think about it. If sex did work to start labor, there would be very few overdue babies, don't you think?

AT THIS POINT

Keep your big maternity bra on

You might have heard that nipple stimulation might also get things moving. While studies have shown that stimulating your nipples by twisting or pinching at this point in your countdown can release oxytocin, other studies have shown that it only helps if your cervix is ripened. Bottom line: There is no conclusive evidence that it works, and prolonged contractions at this point could stress your baby, which will definitely stress you and your S.O., so don't try this one at home!

4 days past due date

ADVICE FROM THE TRENCHES
Oh, yeah, you'll try anything

"With Sophia, my first, I was four days late, and with Ava, believe it or not I had to be induced, as I was approaching two weeks late. I tried every myth to get Ava moving. Sex every day (which, if I may be blunt, included nipple stimulation). Let me say, sex at 9 months ain't comfortable. I drank raspberry tea. I took shower after shower. I walked everywhere. I saw a chiropractor who thought maybe my pelvis was out of line so if I got it adjusted the baby would just slide out . . . not!"
—Dawn, mom to Sophia and Ava

AT THIS POINT
Will your couple mojo ever come back?

You may be wondering, and your S.O. is definitely wondering, if you'll ever willingly have sex again after your pregnancy is over.

According to a poll of seventeen thousand men and three thousand women conducted by BabyCenter.com, the answer for nearly 60 percent of the couples was "yes." Sadly, the other 40 percent found that their sex life got less satisfying. It's hard to be sexy when you're dealing with a baby all day.

ADVICE FROM THE TRENCHES
A new normal

"Your before baby normal sex life no longer applies. You have to work on a new normal now. After the baby, I was just too tired at night. So now when the baby naps . . . After her naps end, we'll come up with another new normal."
—Anonymous mom

5 days past due date

THE WHOLE TRUTH AND NOTHING BUT
Mojo in six weeks?

You may feel a lot better six weeks after giving birth, but with your traumatized vagina or C-section soreness, it can take a whole lot longer than six weeks to recover your body after the transforming experience of childbirth.

The "six weeks and you're normal" urban legend came into being because six weeks is when most women see their doctor for their final postpartum check-up. Six weeks is the average amount of time it takes for your uterus to go back to its normal size, but that may be just about the only thing that goes back to normal for several more months.

Because by then doctors say it's okay to have sex again, people (okay, men) have gotten the idea that you'll actually *want* to have sex again. You may want to have sex again—but then again, you may not. Give yourself time to heal without any expectations of a deadline.

ADVICE FROM THE TRENCHES
You've got to be kidding me

"I had a 9.5-pound (4.3-kg) baby with a head in the ninetieth percentile. I delivered him vaginally after pushing for two and a half hours. I told my husband, 'I don't care what the doctor says at my six-week check-up, sex is so far off my radar screen, in three months I'm still going to need a six-pack and a porno movie to get it back."
—Ellen, mom to Christopher

6 days past due date

HOW TO EAT TO INDUCE LABOR

You may have heard that one way to get labor started is by eating eggplant Parmesan. This story started with a news report about women in Smyrna, Georgia, going into labor within forty-eight hours of eating the eggplant at a restaurant called Scalini's. In fact, the owners now have more than three hundred pictures of babies supposedly born after their mothers ate the eggplant.

So if you don't live in Georgia, try making it at home or visiting your favorite Italian restaurant. What do you have to lose?

TO-DO LIST
Make a pregnancy salad

Another pregnancy food myth sweeping the Internet, or the real thing?

Supposedly, if you combine equal parts romaine lettuce, watercress, and red cabbage with balsamic vinegar dressing and crumbled gorgonzola cheese, you will soon go into labor. However, many women eat balsamic vinegar dressing all along, so this is another one that probably won't work. But at least it's lunch.

THE WHOLE TRUTH AND NOTHING BUT
Stimulating your bowels

You know you're getting desperate if you're thinking about castor oil. Castor oil is a strong laxative. Though stimulating your bowels can cause some uterine contractions, no conclusive studies show that it really works, and it's really, really unpleasant. You only have a few more days—why put yourself through it?

DOCTOR'S ORDERS
Your doctor may strip your membranes

"At some point, in an effort to 'move things along' and get your cervix in the mood for delivery, your doctor or midwife may perform a procedure called stripping or sweeping your membranes.

"Your doctor or midwife inserts his or her finger into your cervix and then sweeps it in a circular motion. This sweeping motion separates the amniotic sac from the opening of the cervix and lower uterine segment.

"At best, it's uncomfortable because of the pressure. At worst, it's very painful. But it's quick—a thirty-second procedure—and it may jumpstart your labor within twenty-four hours. If your doctor recommends this procedure, ask him or her to discuss the pros and cons before you decide."
—K.N.

ADVICE FROM THE TRENCHES
The pain is worth it!

"I've had three children, and I had my membranes stripped with each one because I could only get to two or three centimeters and then I would stay there and not budge. I went into labor within hours of each procedure. For me the discomfort was worth it."
—Tracy, mom to Jake, Paul, and Shannon

8 days past due date

DOCTOR'S ORDERS
What will happen at this week's check-up?

"Once you're a week past your due date, your doctor or midwife will give you a non-stress test, which monitors your baby's heart rate while she's resting and while she's moving for approximately twenty minutes. Just as your heart beats faster when you're active, your baby's should, too. An ultrasound will also be done to see if the amount of amniotic fluid is adequate.

"If your baby doesn't pass the non-stress test, don't panic. Your doctor will then do a special ultrasound called a biophysical profile, which checks your baby's body and breathing movements and the level of amniotic fluid surrounding her. If your baby scores well on this, everything is fine. Your doctor will most likely discuss a plan for induction if you don't begin labor on your own by the end of this week."
—K.N.

TO-DO LIST
Change your voicemail greeting

"Sorry I can't come to the phone right now, but if you were going to ask me if I have had the baby yet, I was going to have to kill you. Don't you think you would have heard if I had had the baby?"

9 days past due date

DOCTOR'S ORDERS
How labor is medically induced

"If your cervix is soft and dilated then it is ripe and ready for labor. Rupturing the amniotic sac—uncomfortable, but usually not painful—can sometimes get your contractions going. Pitocin is usually started at the same time.

"If your cervix is not yet ready, your doctor may try one of many techniques to help ripen it prior to starting pitocin. Some doctors choose to insert a prostaglandin medication (such as cervidil) around the cervix; this medication is left in place for ten to twelve hours. While it usually only softens the cervix, it can sometimes stimulate labor.

"There is also a medication, Cytotec or misoprostol, that can help initiate labor, which can be placed vaginally or taken orally every four to six hours.

"Some doctors insert a Foley catheter into your cervix with a very small balloon at the end of it. When the balloon is inflated with water, it puts pressure on your cervix, stimulating the release of prostaglandins, which will cause it to open and soften. When your cervix begins to dilate, the balloon falls out and the catheter is removed."
—K.N.

ADVICE FROM THE TRENCHES
The purpose of being overdue

"I was very fearful about labor throughout my whole pregnancy. But after I hit week 41, I really got to my breaking point with wanting this pregnancy over and my baby out, no matter how much it hurt. Psychologically, being late made me less afraid."
—Margaret, mom to Shane and Colleen

10 days past due date

HOW TO TELL WHEN A PREGNANT WOMAN IS READY TO BE INDUCED

You know you're overdue—way overdue—when you:

* are wearing one pair of maternity pants and just changing your shirt to that other shirt.

* have only two emotions now—hate and more hate.

* know why there's no Maternity Barbie or Birthing Partner Ken.

* feel freakishly huge—and yet, if someone tells you you're small, you ironically, but perfectly understandably, hate that person's guts.

DOCTOR'S ORDERS
What are the risks with induction?

"Your biggest risk is that induction won't work. So you may end up delivering with a C-section. This can be a difficult, emotional blow, especially if you have gone through three days of a trial of labor.

"Some of the medications used in induction can cause very strong uterine contractions, which can in turn cause stress for the baby, so you will have to be monitored very closely and will have restricted movement. But you have to remember that the monitoring is what will allow your doctor to ensure your health, your baby's health, and a positive outcome."

—K.N.

11 days past due date

AT THIS POINT
You need to know about the "baby blues"

Naturally, when you're overdue, you're miserable, impatient, and pretty much could cry all the time. This is the "overdue blues." Next to follow are the "baby blues."

You think—and expect—that having a baby will be the most joyous time of your life. And it is—at times. But along with the joy of your new baby comes the baby blues—weepiness, loneliness, feelings of inadequacy, vulnerability, and fears that you can't handle motherhood or that you'll do something wrong.

The American National Mental Health Association estimates that 80 percent of all new moms experience the baby blues and that it stems from (what else?) hormonal surges, fatigue, and a difficult transitional time for every woman and couple. These blues usually hit a few days postpartum and usually subside within two weeks.

THE WHOLE TRUTH AND NOTHING BUT
If your baby blues get worse

If the blues don't subside, or you become sad, anxious, despairing, or have disturbing thoughts, you may actually have postpartum depression (PDD). PPD can be a serious condition, but it's very treatable if you seek help. The NMHA estimates that 10 to 20 percent of all new moms suffer from PPD—that translates to hundreds of thousands of women. So if it happens to you, know that you're not alone.

12 days past due date

TO-DO LIST
Put this phone number on your fridge: 1-800-PPD-MOMS

This is a good phone number to have handy—just in case. You can call or visit www.1800ppdmoms.org for help in recognizing and dealing with PPD. This confidential organization offers telephone support from real moms who suffered through it and are now healthy and trained to help other moms. Don't worry, no one will think you're crazy or an unfit mother.

THE WHOLE TRUTH AND NOTHING BUT
Your last chance to sleep

It's so hard to relax after your due date passes, but try to get some sleep now while you still can. As you will discover in a few days, a hospital is no place for an exhausted woman.

Major sleep deprivation begins in your third trimester and continues right into your hospital stay. Even if you're not breastfeeding, your nurses will pressure you to do all of the nightly feedings. And even if you convince them (or get your doctor to write on your chart) that you need sleep and will have tons of practice doing 4 A.M. feedings at home, a nurse or aid will still come in and periodically check your vitals. Even if you manage to sleep through that, your painkillers will wear off, or you'll have to pee and change your pad again. Any time you have your baby in bed with you, you may doze off only to awake in horror that you may have elbowed your baby!

13 days past due date

AT THIS POINT
One child is enough! Way more than enough!

No explanations needed on this one, though you really might change your mind. If no one recovered from the hardships of the third (and fourth) trimesters, no one would have more than one child.

ADVICE FROM THE TRENCHES
Surviving new motherhood . . .

"As far as surprises, I didn't realize parenting would be such a guessing game. Why is she crying? Gas? Hunger? Wet diaper? Teething? Ear infection? It's a constant interactive puzzle, and once you finally figure out all your baby's signs, she changes them."
—Susan, mom to Ian and Oona

"As soon as you can drive, get out of your house and find other new moms. Stroll your neighborhood. Join a playgroup right away. You need other new moms to survive."
—Cindi, mom to Ryan and Claire

"Make sure to take time to eat—I would go from one thing to another with the baby and all of a sudden it would be dinnertime, and I would realize that I had eaten next to nothing all day."
—Michelle, mom to Emily

"In the beginning, have very low expectations of what you will be able to get done, maybe two things a day. One is a shower."
—Clare, mom to Annie and Grace

"Know that your husband will have his own way of doing things, and you'll fight because you'll want him to do it your way. You'll be a little crazy about your way in the beginning!"
—Wanda, mom to Tyree and Shanta

14 days past due date

ADVICE FROM THE TRENCHES
There is no failure

"I've read that some women consider a C-section, and even induction, a failure. How can you be a failure if your cervix wouldn't budge, or if your baby was breech, or if her heartbeat dropped? Just be grateful for your healthy baby!"
—Jen, mom to Jack and Madison

THE WHOLE TRUTH AND NOTHING BUT
So it didn't go according to plan

Okay, so you didn't feel a big bang of a contraction on your due date. You didn't head to the hospital and find an anesthesiologist waiting to give you an epidural. And you didn't deliver your baby thirty minutes later while eating a turkey sandwich.

No one gets the birth they had imagined. Because childbirth is almost impossible to imagine. Remember how you thought you knew what pregnancy would be like? And now look at you!

AT THIS POINT
One door closes (after you've squeezed through it)

Here is your official, slightly early welcome to the next club—a club so hugely different it's like finding yourself on a new planet—Planet Motherhood.

On Planet Motherhood, nothing ever goes the way you think it will. At times it is harder than you had ever imagined, but ultimately it is a journey so full of love and transformation, you will wonder what gave your life meaning before.

In less than twenty-four hours, you are going to be a mother, and you're going to be great!

Index and Acknowledgments

Index

Index

Acknowledgments

Though you rarely write any book without help, I really had a lot of help with this one. To all of the women who shared their pregnancy experiences with me, I thank you. (To all of the strangers I approached in grocery stores: See, I wasn't just a crazy woman, I really was writing a book.)

First and foremost, thank you Dr. Kara Nakisbendi. You are a very cool person and it makes me happy to know that doctors like you exist. I could not have done this book without you.

Next, I would like to thank all of the women in my moms' group. In particular I am especially grateful to Jen McDougall, Marianne Marquet, Dawn Poeta, and Alison Walton for sharing so generously and honestly.

I would like to thank my publisher, Dave Borgenicht, for "getting" this book and allowing me to write it. When I knew Dave way back when, it was clear then he would one day build his own very successful publishing empire. It's no surprise to me that he did and that he's still one of the nicest guys in town.

To my very talented editor, Jason Rekulak, father of one, I owe a great debt of thanks. When this book became like a real pregnancy—much harder than I thought it would be and way overdue—Jason hung in there with me.

Thank you to Quirk's managing editor, Erin Slonaker, for her tremendous help in pulling it all together. Also, a big thanks to Jon Barthmus at Skidmutro Creative + Layout for the book's fun design. It's perfect!

Finally, I wish to thank my sisters, Kathy (Kate) Holemans and Clare Daniels, for showing me how to be a mother, helping me keep it real, and for keeping me laughing on the hard days.